LIKE A PEBBLE TOSSED
The Legacy of a Prayer

By

Jean Lovelace Zeiler
with Mayo Mathers

To Billie — Thank you for the delightful week at Salishan. 7-15-00 Betty Love

ACW Press
5501 N. 7th Ave. #502
Phoenix, AZ 85013

Publisher's Cataloging-in-Publication
(Provided by Quality Books, Inc.)

Zeiler, Jean Lovelace.
 Like a pebble tossed : the legacy of a prayer / by
Jean Zeiler with Mayo Mathers.
 p. cm.
 ISBN 1-892525-03-8

 1. Zeiler, Jean Lovelace. 2. Judges--Oregon--
Biography. 3. Women judges--Oregon--Biography.
 4. Ranchers--Oregon--Biography. 5. Women ranchers-

Oregon--Biography. 6. Actresses--New York (State)--
New York--Biography. 7. Spiritual biography.
 I. Title

KF373.Z45A3 1998   347.795'014'092 [B]
                          QBI98-1148

Printed in the United States of America

To obtain more copies please contact:
Mayo Mathers
20129 Mathers Rd.,
Bend, OR 97701
See the order form in the back of this book.

Some names have been changed to protect their privacy.

Dedication

To Ivan Saunders, a gentle, quiet man, whose faith
ignited a flame in my heart for Jesus Christ.

To Reverend Enns who encouraged and challenged me
to fan the flame that Ivan sparked.

Acknowledgments

I wish to thank Steve Laube, my editor, whose expertise and humor has made the publication of my first book such a joyful experience. I also wish to thank my pastor, Randy Myers, and my Bible Study group who have been an unceasing source of encouragement. And a special thanks to my friend and chess partner, Dennis DeHaan of Radio Bible Class, for his late night telephone call from a phone booth in Boston urging me to pursue publication of this book.

Contents

About the Authors

Jean Zeiler and Mayo Mathers are both widely traveled conference and retreat speakers who met many years ago when Jean and her husband bought a ranch in eastern Oregon that was adjacent to Mayo's grandmother's ranch. Jean's stories from her career as an actress enchanted Mayo when she was a child and when they met again years later they decided to weave the stories into a book.

Mayo Mathers is a columnist for *Today's Christian Woman* and a freelance writer whose work has appeared in many publications including, *Focus on the Family, Guideposts, Virtue, Decision* and *Moody*. She has been a contributing writer for five books published by Multnomah Press and Tyndale House Publishers. Her work is featured on the "Family Radio News," a national broadcast centered in Oakland, California.

Prologue

His name was Ivan Saunders, and he was an engineer in the firm where I worked as a draftsman. There was nothing particularly outstanding about him; he was sandy haired, slightly pudgy, and of medium height. He wore conservative, wire-rimmed glasses to match his quiet, unassuming manner. He was also a Christian.

Every day at noon Ivan bowed his head and prayed over his brown lunch sack. I watched him relentlessly, waiting for the day he would forget to pray. "Christian Watching" was my hobby. I waited for them to "drop the ball," and inevitably, they did. *Ah ha!* I'd think gleefully when this happened, *I'm as good as they are! I don't need anything they've got.*

But in all the months I watched Ivan, he never forgot to say his prayer. And although he never expressed his faith to me in words, his life spoke volumes. Ivan had something the rest of us lacked.

One day, I walked over to Ivan's desk to question him about the current high-rise apartment complex we were working on. A couple of the engineers were with me.

"Ivan, just off the top of your head, do you think this size pump can really lift that much pressure seventeen stories?"

He smiled and reached behind his desk for a large book of specifications. Ivan never did things "off the top of his head."

"Well, Fellas," I joked to the engineers, "we'll have to wait until Ivan checks his 'Bible.'" They all guffawed as I knew they would, but Ivan's hand froze on the book he had just opened.

"Jean," he said softly, "this is not my Bible."

All laughter ceased, and an awkward silence settled around the desk. I felt awful. My flippant comment had hurt him.

Ivan's quiet response sent me to a bookstore the very next day. I decided to see for myself what a Bible like Ivan's had to say. It seems impossible that something as insignificant as praying before lunch could have had such a profound effect on me, but it did. Ivan's silent and consistent witness, day after day, eventually led me to Christ.

It took me a long time to get there. Many pathways had to be searched and many thoughts and emotions explored, before I learned the difference between religion and a relationship with God.

Chapter One
A Childhood Ringed in Magic

By the time I was a freshman in high school, I had attended eighteen different schools. Dad's job as a cattle buyer for the Portland (Oregon) Stockyards sent him traipsing back and forth across the western states searching out the best livestock buys.

My mother, my sister Iris, and I never minded the variety of places we lived on the road. Sometimes it was an apartment, a rooming house, or even a tent. I thought it was a wonderful way to live and never minded not having a real home like other children. We were a family, and that was all that mattered to me.

One spring, when I was four and Iris almost six, Daddy put his carpentry skills to work and built us a house on wheels in preparation for an extended trip through fifteen western states. This was long before motor homes.

Using a two-ton truck chassis, he built and attached a small rectangular room to it. The result looked much like a bus. In the front, next to the driver's seat, he bolted an easy chair to the floor for Mama. Iris and I sat in two chairs fastened down close behind them. We had a trunk, closet, and cupboard for storage, and in the back, Daddy built a full-sized bunk bed for our sleeping quarters. Iris and I slept on top and Daddy and Mama on the bottom. To "fancy" things up Mama sewed a pretty curtain to hang across the beds for privacy. To complete our home, Daddy crafted a table that folded down from the side wall, where we gathered to eat, read, and play games.

As we traveled, we stopped along the way to bathe in suitable places, and hauled water for other needs in a big milk can. Occasionally, Daddy stopped the truck next to a park, and while he and Mama relaxed, Iris and I went off to play. One time we stopped at a small city park somewhere in Wyoming.

Catching sight of a swing set, Iris and I took off across the grass squealing in delight. We each jumped into a swing and began pumping furiously to see who could get the highest. Just as we were growing tired, a man walked over and began to help by giving us each a push. This made it even more fun.

Soon we were out of breath from swinging and laughing, and we began to let our swings slow down. Suddenly, the man grabbed Iris's arm. Startled, she let out a little yelp.

"If ya want me to let your sister go," he leered at me, "ya gotta give me a kiss!"

I stared at him in shock, not knowing what to do. I didn't want to kiss him, but I didn't want him to hurt Iris, either.

"Come on, Little Girlie," he persisted, "just one little kiss, and I'll let your sister go."

I looked at Iris and saw tears coming down her cheeks. A determined fury swelled up in me. I stepped closer to give him a kiss, but as I leaned toward him, I suddenly kicked him as hard as I could, screaming with all the force my lungs could muster. Startled, the man let go of Iris, and we raced across the grass toward our truck, shrieking in terror. Instantly, Daddy appeared in the doorway. As we pointed toward the man now hurrying away, he gave chase.

It seemed like he was gone forever. While we waited for him to return, Mama made sure Iris wasn't hurt and then calmed us both down. When Daddy finally climbed into the truck, his face was grim. He shushed away our questions and started the motor. Iris and I never did find out if he caught up with that man, but in my heart, I knew he had. Daddy was my hero.

He had a way of teaching us important lessons in life so we weren't even aware of being taught. One lesson I particularly remember came when I was five years old, and Daddy gently gave me a glimpse of what it was like to be an adult.

We were living in a rented house at the time. Daddy had been watching me run along the fence next to a meadow where there was a long line of telephone poles. I ran from the first pole to the second one, then ran all the way back. Stopping right in front of him, I bragged, "Betcha can't beat me."

Daddy laughed and agreed that I did run awfully fast. "Don't you just love to run?" I said, jumping up and down happily.

Daddy wasn't sure about that, but said he used to run almost as much as me and every bit as fast.

"Betcha can't run as fast as me now!" I challenged.

Daddy smiled. "Okay, let's race, and we'll see."

I wanted to start right then, but I was still panting from my last run, and Daddy insisted we wait a few minutes. I tried to calm down, but kept giggling in anticipation. Finally Daddy said we could start.

"I'll tell you what," he said, "because I have longer legs than you, maybe I should give you a head start. You go up to the next telephone pole, and I'll stay here. When I say 'go,' we'll both race to the third pole. And I bet I'll beat you!"

I was so excited! Nobody could beat me with that much of a head start—not even Daddy. I ran off to my pole and looked back.

"Are you ready?" he hollered. I nodded hard and giggled. "On your mark!" he called. "Get set......GO!"

I shot forward. Only the distance of one pole; Daddy had two. This would be so easy. I giggled and looked back. He was running fast, maybe even catching up a little. I put more effort into my sprint. Now I was flying over the ground. *Nobody could catch me.*

I was halfway there when Daddy called, "I'm gaining on you!" I glanced back. He'd passed my beginning pole and was coming fast. My heart and lungs pounded with determination as I raced on. *I just had to beat him!* Tears came to my eyes. *I had to—it was only a little farther...*

Suddenly I saw Daddy's shadow right behind me. *He was almost up to me!* I could hardly catch my breath. *Just a little more.* We were neck and neck now, the finish pole just a few steps away. All at once, Daddy stepped ahead and touched the pole. I was only a second behind him, but he won...and as he turned to face me, he was laughing.

I realized then that he could have beat me all the time. He wasn't even breathing hard. I had run my legs off, given it everything I had, and Daddy hadn't even had to try.

I didn't cry. We just stood there and looked at each other, and it was such a long, sad look. I could tell Daddy was sorry, too. He saw how much he'd hurt me. *If he just hadn't laughed.*

He reached out and touched my cheek. "It's all right, Honey. You did real good."

I just kept staring at him. I would remember that moment forever; something seemed to die in me a little. *When he knew all along he could beat me, why had he let me try so hard?*

That night I woke up crying. I had been dreaming about our *race*. I laid there staring up at the ceiling and thought, *Someday I'll be all grown up, and I'll have a little girl just like me. And sometimes we'll play together, and when we do, I'll never laugh when I beat her in a game.* I began to cry again.

Suddenly, Daddy appeared by my side. He leaned over my bed and put his hand on my cheek, feeling the tears. Grabbing me up into his arms he asked, "What's wrong, Honey? Do you hurt?" He carried me out to his big chair by the fireplace. Mama was there mending clothes and she looked up with concern. I gulped and sniffled, trying to stop crying. Daddy didn't say anything for a long time, and then he asked, "Did you have a bad dream, Punkin? Do you want to tell me about it? Sometimes it helps to talk."

I fiddled with one of the buttons on his shirt. "Our race..."

Daddy looked sadly over at Mama and hugged me again. "Oh, Jeannie, Jeannie," he sighed, "it's hard growing up, isn't it?" He got out his handkerchief and made me blow my nose. Mama laid down her sewing and pulled her rocker over real close to Daddy's chair. "Let Daddy try to explain," he said. "I've thought a lot about our race. I guess you have, too." He glanced again at Mama. "You really haven't been running too long, have you, Honey?"

"I guess not," I snuffled.

"Well, Daddy's been running for a long time, and when we had our race this afternoon I really had a hard time, too. You see, I wanted you to win so much. In fact, I almost let you win, but somehow it would have been like cheating or lying. Do you know what I mean?" His arms still held me snug against him. "Jeannie, you were being so honest in your race, and you raced really good for being five years old. But would you rather I let you win, or would you rather really and truly win?"

I didn't know. I honestly didn't know. What I did know was that Daddy and Mama were hurting, too. Mama got down on her knees by the chair and put her arms around me. I sucked in my breath real hard to keep from crying again.

"Well," I snuffled, "I guess as long as I did real good, it was good enough, wasn't it?"

Daddy tilted my chin back and looked right into my eyes. "Honey, your best is all anybody can ever ask of you. You did your best, and it was fine." Then he looked at Mama, and they smiled at each other. "Our little girl is growing up," Daddy said.

Another lesson Daddy taught me had to do with swearing, something Iris and I were forbidden to do. We'd been playing outside one afternoon when Iris got mad at me and did just that.

"Daddy!" I yelled, running into the house. "Iris swore at me!"

Looking up from his work he said, "So?"

"But Daddy! You told us never to swear!"

"I see," he said thoughtfully. "Well, what do you think I should do about it?"

Daddy's calm reaction to my dramatic news puzzled me. "You should *spank* her!" I insisted.

By this time, Iris had come into the room and stood there with her arms crossed defiantly over her chest.

"Okay." Daddy's voice was resigned. "Both of you go pick out a piece of kindling for me to spank Iris with."

This was not going at all the way I had planned. Still, I was determined that Iris be punished for swearing at me. Together, we trudged down to the basement where the kindling was stacked. At first I grabbed the biggest stick I could find, but when I held it up, my determination began to waver. I sorted through the pile for a medium-sized one. All the while Iris stared stony-faced. Finally I threw back the medium piece, grabbed a small one and headed back up the stairs, Iris on my heels.

"Is this the stick you want me to use?" Daddy asked as he held it up to examine. Upstairs, it looked much larger than it had in the basement.

"Yes." I said, but my voice was losing its strength.

"Are you sure?"

I nodded mutely.

"Okay then. Iris, come here and bend over." Iris walked over to Daddy and bent over. Then he dramatically raised his hand high in the air.

"STOP!" I shrieked.

Daddy paused and looked at me. "But Jeannie, I can't stop. You told me Iris broke the rules, and now she has to be punished." He slowly raised his hand again.

"NO!" I cried. "I was bad, too. I tattled, and you tell us we shouldn't tattle either."

"Hm-m-m-m," said Daddy thoughtfully. "You're right. What should I do now?"

"Spank *her*, Daddy!" said Iris, thankful for her reprieve.

Daddy ignored her. "I guess there is only one thing to do," he said, looking at us both with great sadness. "You girls are going to have to spank me."

We stared at him astounded. *"WHAT?"* we said in unison."

"I'm a bad daddy. I have a daughter who swears and a daughter who tattles. You must each give me three swats with this piece of kindling."

I stared at the stick in horror. This episode was turning out very badly. I surely didn't want to hit Daddy with the piece of kindling I had chosen for Iris.

We both began weeping copiously, but Daddy bent over and insisted we swat him. Reluctantly we each barely touched the stick to his leg, but he cried out in apparent pain.

Mama, who had been standing in the doorway, watching the whole procedure, came over to him. "There, there," she soothed as she led him out of the room, leaving Iris and me alone to consider our behavior. Swearing and tattling were never an issue after that.

And thus it was with all the other issues of our life. Daddy and Mama were always there to show us a better way. For me, our childhood was ringed in magic. Every day brought new adventures, woven through by a sturdy cord of love. But it was not to last.

Jean and her sister, Iris
(Jean got to hold the toy)

Chapter Two
A Barrage of Tragedies

Late one summer our parents rented a house in the northeast Park Rose district of Portland. Iris wasn't feeling very well, and they thought it best not to travel until she got better. At first it seemed like she just had the flu, but soon her whole body ached. When she tried to walk, her legs wobbled, and then refused to hold her up at all. Day and night, Mama stayed in Iris's room trying to nurse her back to health. It hurt her to swallow, so Mama and Daddy took turns playing simple games with her to coax her to eat small bites of Jell-O or bread soaked in milk.

In between feeding her, Mama massaged Iris's thinning arms and legs, trying to soothe her misery, yet she continued to grow worse. Soon Iris was unable to move. A pall of fear fell over our house. It seemed as if everyone had lost the ability to speak out loud.

Since we didn't know if Iris's illness was contagious, I was not allowed to go to school. At home, I was banned from her room. Without Iris I was lost and, for the first time in my life, couldn't think of anything to do. Mama and Daddy were so preoccupied with Iris's care, I felt invisible. My only companion was Fluffy, our toy collie dog, and we spent our days huddled together in quiet misery.

Once or twice a day I was allowed to stand in the doorway of Iris's room and say hello. After one very long, lonely day, I took Fluffy to the doorway. Holding her up so Iris could see her I cried, "Iris, if you'll just get well and come out to play with me, I'll give you my half of Fluffy!"

Iris couldn't even turn her head, but her eyes brightened at the sight of our pet. The tips of her fingers motioned weakly in our direction. I set Fluffy down on the floor, and she bounded happily across the room and up onto the bed to Iris.

"No!" Mama cried, and moved to scoot Fluffy off, but a small whimper from Iris stopped her. Fluffy lay down beside Iris and licked her fingers. From that moment on Fluffy rarely left Iris's side. Mama even set her bowl of food and water by the bed, so she wouldn't have to leave. Now I was completely alone.

By this time we knew Iris had the dreaded disease, infantile paralysis, also known as polio. For many weeks she fought against it as it twisted and deformed her small body. For three days she hovered on the brink of death. Then at last she began to show signs of improvement.

Her recovery was long and painful, and she had to learn to walk all over again. My once active, rambunctious sister now slithered from room to room like a snake, drooling and making inhuman guttural sounds, as yet unable to speak. Years later Mom confessed to me. "Jean, I used to look at your sister and pray to God she'd either get well or die. I couldn't stand seeing her like that."

Like a baby learning to walk, Iris used a chair to pull herself up to a standing position by the table. Hanging on to the edge with a death grip she refused to let anyone help her. "No!" she'd growl fiercely through her weakened vocal cords. Sometimes, as we stood by helplessly, she gritted her teeth so hard that blood trickled from her mouth.

In many ways, polio changed the fabric of our family. It left Iris flatfooted, with a weak right leg so she never walked normally again. Without realizing what we were doing, Mom, Dad, and I fell into the habit of trying to compensate for her circumstances. Out of love, we coddled her, even as an adult, and it began to create a chasm in our relationship.

Once, many years later, when Mom and Iris came to visit me, Mom took me aside and whispered, "Jean, let's do things Iris's way while we're all together. We can do it 'our' way after she leaves, okay?" For some reason, that really hurt me.

That year while she was ill, Iris and I didn't attend much school. The next fall, when I entered school, I soon began to flounder, unable to keep up with the other students my age. To my immense humiliation, I was held back a grade. Fortunately, my teacher was a kind woman who seemed to realize how traumatic the setback was for me.

During art class one day, I drew a picture of some flowers. My teacher realized that my drawing ability was quite advanced for my age. Thinking it might perk up my self esteem, she had me take my drawing down the hall to show my former classmates. Her plan backfired miserably. As I walked around the class displaying my art work, I could hear the kids snickering and whispering. My face flamed hot, and I couldn't wait to leave the room. I cried all the way home from school that day.

Our parents decided to give Iris tap dancing lessons in hopes of strengthening her leg muscles. I longed to take lessons too, but Dad could only afford to pay for one of us. I decided I didn't need any lessons to learn how to dance; I would just copy Iris. I accompanied her to almost every lesson, watching intently, memorizing the steps as the teacher taught them to her.

At home I practiced tirelessly, savoring the feel of my body as it responded to the rhythm of the music on our phonograph. The movements came naturally to me, and I soon progressed beyond Iris. The teacher became aware of what I was doing and convinced our parents I should take lessons also. A deal was struck between them that was affordable for Dad. Later, I helped pay for my lessons by teaching beginning students for her.

One night Mom and Dad took us to a stage show at the Paramount Theater. Enraptured, I watched the acrobatic dancers perform, memorizing their magical movements. The seeds of a dream began to take root in my heart, and I nudged Mom. "Someday, I'm going to do that!" I whispered to her. She smiled and patted my hand.

Back at home, I went upstairs and began to dance the way I had seen the performers do. One of their most impressive routines had included a backward chest roll. Thinking I could do it too, I copied what I had seen them do. However, I neglected to turn my head sideways when going into the roll and split my nose wide open. I lost a lot of blood that night, but none of my enthusiasm. I was more determined than ever to become a dancer...and maybe even an actress.

A love for the dramatic guided my life. I once wrote my own play, dragging the neighborhood children into my cast. We gave a backyard performance for our parents, charging them five cents admission. Their accommodating applause was exhilarating. I loved it—and wanted more!

While we were living in Tigard, Oregon, I first became aware of God. We lived across the road from a girl named Lillian who was eight years old. Lillian was lucky enough to have her very own, little room in the attic of her home. Iris and I always had to share a room. The tiny, narrow space Lillian had to herself seemed like heaven to me. In one corner, she had set up a little altar where she prayed each day. I admired the small statue of the Madonna sitting on a shelf between two candles that Lillian lit when she prayed. She was the only religious person I knew, and since she was Catholic, I figured only Catholics were Christians. It was at that private little altar that a hunger for God took root within my heart.

A year later, when we moved back to Portland, I began attending Sunday School with my next door neighbor, a girl named Clara. This was my first experience with "religion," and I loved it. I memorized all my Sunday School verses and devoured the Bible stories. God sounded so wonderful to me, but He also seemed so very far away.

Clara quit going to Sunday School, but I continued on my own. I went for an entire year without missing once. One morning my teacher announced there would be a special ceremony the following Sunday to recognize all those who had perfect attendance for the past year. "Jean," she said, smiling at me, "you're one of those who will be recognized. Next Sunday you will be given a very special pin."

All that week, I could hardly wait for Sunday to arrive. By Saturday night I was too excited to even sleep. I got up the next morning and dressed very carefully, wanting to look my very best for such a special occasion.

At church, I sat upstairs in the main sanctuary along with all the other children as the service began. One by one, the children's names were called, and they walked forward to the pulpit. I soon realized, however, that something was terribly wrong. As the children walked to the front, their parents came to join them. My parents weren't there. I sat in the pew in abject misery, terrified I wouldn't be given a pin when everyone realized I was alone. When my name was called, I walked nervously to the front.

The pastor stared down at me. "Where are your parents?" he asked.

"They couldn't come," I mumbled.

To my immense relief, the pastor didn't refuse me a pin. With great tenderness he leaned down to pin it on my dress, then shook my hand just as he had done with all the others. How proud I was at that moment, even though I stood there alone. I didn't realize that this was the first of many times when I would stand alone on important occasions, with none of my family to support or encourage me.

When I was ten years old, we moved to Oak Grove, a suburb of Portland. Our house there was a large, two-story structure with a wraparound porch. Just inside the front door, a small spiral staircase led to the second story. At the top of the stairs were two bedrooms and a small sewing room. To my intense delight, Mom said the sewing room could be my bedroom. There was a window in one wall that looked out over a smooth, green lawn. At night, I'd kneel there, looking up at the stars and dreaming of the day I would be an actress or a professional dancer. Nothing seemed impossible to me. I would make it happen...someday.

It was there, in the fifth grade, that I first saw Roy Zeiler. I was playing softball on the school playground when he and another boy rode by on their bikes.

They stopped to watch the game for a few moments, and Roy asked his buddy, "Who's that girl in the white middy?"

"That's Jean Lovelace. She's new here."

"Well," said Roy, smiling in admiration, "I'm going to go with her someday."

I heard about Roy's comment through the school grape-vine, but didn't actually meet him until the following summer down at Oak Grove Beach, on the Willamette River, where all the kids met to swim. It was everyone's goal to swim across the river to the multilevel refueling dock for barges and steam-boats—a perfect place to practice diving.

I had been swimming with Roy for several weeks be-fore I realized he was the one who had bragged he would "go with me someday." Our friendship developed that summer and through the following school years. Occasionally, Roy showed up at my house to walk me to school or give me a ride on his bike. He was nice enough, but I wasn't terribly impressed with him. He was tall and skinny—practically all bones—and he had a huge Adam's apple protruding from his scrawny neck. *Not the best catch in the world*, I thought. But he made a terrific friend, and since I was a tomboy, we had great times hiking, climbing trees, swimming, and playing ball together.

Now as I look back, I realize that Roy was the only constant in my life. From the fifth grade on, through all the twists, turns, and detours, he was there.

I was in the eighth grade when my secure little world was smashed into a million tiny pieces, never to be put back together again. One day, as I sat at my school desk, a noise at the back of the room caught my attention. Mom was standing in the classroom doorway. Surprised, I looked at my teacher, and he nodded his head in dismissal. Gathering up my books, I walked toward Mom. She'd never before come to my school, and whatever had brought her here now, I knew couldn't be good.

Something about her kept me from asking questions, and we walked in silence down the endless school corridor. Dread echoed in the click of her heels on the wooden floor. Outside, Dad and Iris were waiting for us in the car. As I slid into the back seat next to Iris, I shot a questioning glance at her, but she only gave me a worried shrug. No one spoke as we drove to our home.

Once inside, Dad said quietly, "Girls, sit down."

We sat down side by side on the davenport, watching our parents. Whatever they had to tell us, we wanted to be together. An awful stillness screamed through the room.

"Your mother and I are no longer in love," Dad said abruptly. "We're getting a divorce."

We stared at him in stunned silence. I looked at Mom. *Surely this was a mistake.* But she looked straight into my eyes and nodded mutely. It was as though someone had walked into our house and shot off a cannon. I sucked in a long, ragged breath. *We were a "family," and families didn't get divorced. We loved each other. We always had. We still did. Dad was wrong!*

A suffocating fog seemed to fill the room. I continued to stare at them in shocked disbelief, but neither Mom nor Dad said anything to erase the words that had just smashed our family to pieces.

After a long pause Mom cleared her throat and said, "I'm going to go into Portland to get a hotel room for the night, girls." Her voice was husky and wavering. "You may come with me if you want."

We walked numbly out of the room without speaking and trudged upstairs to Iris's bedroom. With the door shut behind us we tried to speak, but had trouble finding the words.

"What should we do?" I finally whispered to Iris. The pain inside my heart was too deep for tears. I felt all withered up and hollow.

"I think one of us should stay with Dad and one of us go with Mom," Iris suggested, looking as wretched as I felt. "That way neither of them will be alone." I nodded in agreement.

We decided I would go with Mom, and Iris would stay with Dad. In a deep heaviness and dead silence, Iris helped me pack a few things into my overnight bag, and we walked downstairs to where Mom waited with her suitcase. I couldn't think of anything to say. It was as if someone had turned off all the lights. Dad's face was blank. So was Mom's. I started to go to Dad for a hug, but couldn't. Nothing was right. Mom put her hand on Iris's shoulder for a moment and then just walked out through the front door. I followed her. The sound of that door closing behind us pierced my very soul.

We took the interurban streetcar into downtown Portland. I stared numbly out the window, listening to the clickety-clack of the wheels on the tracks. I felt as though my heart had attached itself to one of the wheels. I longed to cry from the pain of the beating it was taking, but the tears wouldn't come.

We got off on Fourth Street and found a room in a dilapidated old hotel. It was tiny, with faded walls and yellowed paint. One naked light bulb hung down from the ceiling in the middle of the room. I can still see that lone bulb in my mind, garishly lighting that strange place.

Silently, Mom and I began to undress. Suddenly her shoulders began to shake, and I rushed over to her. As sobs wracked her body, I helped her into her nightgown and led her over to the bed. She slumped down wearily while I slid in beside her. Then as she continued to weep, I held her.

"It's all right, Mom," I tried to soothe. "Go ahead and cry. Get it all out."

Mom cried herself to sleep in my arms that night, and as I stared dry-eyed into the darkness, I wondered what would happen to us now. I was sure of only one thing. This whole scene was terribly, horribly wrong. She was the mother; I was the child; and yet tonight I was the mother and she was the child. In the darkness of that awful night I said good-bye to my childhood.

———

The seeds of this devastating divorce were sown many years before, when Dad was very young. He was the fifth of seven children—two girls and five boys. His parents, Marion and Martha Lovelace, owned a thousand-acre dairy farm outside of Chehalis, Washington. Although Dad was very intelligent, he left school after the fifth grade to go to work. He was a muscular, brawny man of medium stature; a born mathematician and jack-of-all-trades, able to do almost any kind of work. His droll sense of humor helped him make friends easily, and in every job he took, he advanced quickly.

When he was seventeen he fell in love with a young woman named Tee, and without a word to anyone, they eloped.

Grandma, who ruled the family, was so furious with her son that she wrote him out of the family will and refused to acknowledge the marriage. It became her fiercest goal to break them up.

Dad and Tee moved into a tiny cabin just east of the dairy farm and set up housekeeping. However, Dad couldn't find any work to support his new wife, who immediately became pregnant. He finally resorted to taking a job at a logging mill forty miles from home. The mill owner was hesitant to hire him for fear he would always be wanting time off to visit his pregnant wife. Dad gave his word he wouldn't go home for three months.

He worked hard those three months, although he was desperately lonely and homesick for Tee. He wrote to her every chance he got, sending her his paychecks so she would have the money she needed for food and supplies. He grew concerned when he received no letters in reply. Each letter home became desperate as he begged her to write and let him know she was all right. He filled page after page with his declarations of love, but still no answer came. There were no phones, no other way to reach her. Sick with worry for Tee, Dad longed to go home, but he kept his word to his employer.

At the end of his three months he picked up his final check and rushed back to Chehalis. He ran up to the door of their little cabin and flung it open. It was empty. Tee was gone. Grandma told him she had gone to Idaho with another man.

Grandma was sure her son would soon recover from his brief love affair, but she was wrong. Dad stayed on at the dairy farm, working for his folks, but for the first time in his life he withdrew from people. Grandpa offered to give him back his share of the farm, but Dad refused. Finally he left the farm and the little cabin, filled with their painful memories.

He moved to Portland, Oregon, and worked at various odd jobs, including one at a tuberculosis sanatorium near Milwaukee. It was there he met my mother, Nellie Wise, and for the first time since Tee, Dad became interested in another woman. Mom's independent, industrious nature matched his own, and as they worked side by side, they began to fall in love. Within a year they were married.

Their life together didn't get off to an easy start. The early years of their marriage were filled with disappointment and grief. They left the sanatorium and moved to Idaho, where they started a wheat ranch with another couple. In spite of their hard work and determination, the forces of nature worked against them in the form of a devastating drought that destroyed their wheat crop. They had no recourse but to walk away from their ranch empty-handed.

They got on a train and headed back to Oregon, where they found a small cabin near St. Helens. Mom's ailing parents soon came to live with them.

The winter of 1916 was cold and relentless. While Dad did odd jobs and looked for permanent work, Mom did what she could to make their crowded cabin homey. The only bright spot was the fact that she was pregnant. At night, while her parents slept, Mom and Dad snuggled together and dreamed of better days to come. The child she carried was their future, and made their present struggle bearable.

During that long, frozen winter, Grandma Wise became very ill with an enlarged heart. Mom cared for her, turning her often to prevent bedsores. Grandma was a large, rawboned woman, and turning her became more and more difficult as Mom's pregnancy progressed. One morning as she struggled to lift Grandma, she felt a sharp, wrenching pain. She bit her lip to keep from crying out, not wanting to upset her mother.

Throughout the afternoon jagged pains formed a vise-like grip around Mom's body. Finally, she dragged herself to the door and called weakly for Dad, who was outside in the snow chopping wood.

Dad heard the panic in her voice and threw down his ax.

"Nell!" he cried, running toward her. "What's wrong?"

"The baby..." she gasped, and collapsed in his arms.

The next morning Dad went outside in the bitter cold. With a shovel he attacked the frozen ground, as tears froze to his cheeks. In one long afternoon and torturous night, they had lost both Grandma and their first child—a son, Jack.

Two farmers passing by, stopped.

"What're you doing?" asked one.

"Digging a grave," replied Dad.

When the men learned what had happened, they got off their wagons and sent Dad back to the cabin. "Let us dig it for you," they said.

The next day they returned for the burial. Dad carried Mom outside and set her down beside the grave. While snow fell around them, they clung to each other and wept as their son was buried in his grandmother's arms. Afterwards, the men insisted that Mom and Dad go back into the cabin while they filled in the grave.

Inside, out of the bitter wind, Dad carried Mom over to the bed to lay her down. As he did, he inadvertently knocked off her glasses. Almost blind without them, Mom reached to catch them, but they slipped from her grasp and shattered on the floor. She and Dad stared down at this latest disaster—then looked at each other and broke into hysterical laughter. A heart can only absorb so much pain—then all that is left is the release of hollow laughter. Later, they wondered what the two farmers had thought when they heard laughter drifting from the cabin on that terrible day.

That was their darkest hour. Soon afterward Dad heard of work at a mill in Portland, and slowly he and Mom got back on their feet. Two-and-one-half years after my brother's death, Iris was born; and eighteen months later, me.

When I was eleven years old, a letter addressed to Dad arrived at our house in Oak Grove. I was too young to interpret the look that came over Dad's face as he stared at the handwriting, or to understand why his hand shook as he opened the envelope. I was certainly too young to grasp how a few simple words scrawled across a piece of paper by someone I had never heard of could have such a devastating effect on our lives. The words Dad read that day became a slashing knife wound that would leave all of us with eternal scars.

"*Floyd,*

I've never bothered to write you before, but I

have four children now, and one, a daughter, is yours.

The least you could do is send her some support occasionally..."

These were the first words Dad had heard from Tee since he had left her to go work in the mill so long ago. He hadn't even known their baby was a girl. Immediately he was awash with feelings of love and betrayal from the past.

Mother, knowing all this had happened before Dad had met her, was very kind and understanding. She agreed Dad should send Tee some money, and he did whenever possible.

Months later another letter arrived, this time from the twenty-year-old daughter he'd never met. She wanted to meet her father. Dad was beside himself with excitement as he waited for her at the train depot in Portland.

All I remember about his daughter's visit was her aloofness to Iris and me and her rudeness to my mother. She wanted nothing to do with us. Dad fawned over her, taking her wherever she wanted to go, trying to make up for the years they had lost. Through it all, Mom remained very understanding about this child from Dad's past.

At the end of her visit, Dad drove his daughter back home to Idaho, taking her to the potato factory where Tee was working. "I knew her from a block and a half away," he told me many years later. "She looked just the same."

When Tee caught sight of Dad, she walked slowly toward him, her eyes locked to his. Her first words were bitter. "Why didn't you write me?"

Dad gasped. "But Tee, I did! Why didn't you write me back?"

"Ha!" Tee snorted derisively. Turning on her heel, she walked to her car and drove off without a backward glance.

Dad headed back to Portland, mulling over Tee's strange accusation. *He'd written her handfuls of letters! How could she not have received them? Why was she so bitter?*

On impulse he took a 150-mile "detour" on the way home. Suddenly he had a hunch about the letters. Pulling up to his parents' farm outside Chehalis, Washington, he stormed into the house. "What did you do with all the letters I wrote to Tee?" he demanded of his surprised mother.

Martha Lovelace's face crumpled into tears as she led him upstairs to the trunk in her bedroom. There at the very bottom were two stacks of letters—one from Floyd to Tee, the other from Tee to Floyd. All Lovelace mail had been put in the same family mailbox, and Grandma had intercepted every single letter they had written to each other.

Dad tore open the envelopes, and all the money and uncashed checks that Tee had never received fell out. Seeing the checks, he realized the horror Tee had lived through in the months he was away. Alone, pregnant, with no money at all, she'd been literally starving to death. No wonder she'd left with the man who had offered to help her. She'd thought Dad had abandoned her.

Gathering up the letters he dashed out of the house, running from the pain he had found there. Later that night, he and Mom read the letters together. For the first time Mom began to understand the depth of love and anguish that had occurred in her husband's first marriage. A chill began to settle around her own heart.

Dad wrote Tee, explaining about the letters his mother had intercepted so long ago. Tee didn't respond. Finally, Dad drove back to Idaho, taking the letters with him—desperate for Tee to understand what had happened. He shoved the letters into her hands, and she stared down at them for a long moment. Finally she looked up at Dad.

"What do these letters change?" she asked bitterly. "We both have other lives now."

"But I feel so bad..." Dad countered.

"Well, there's nothing we can do about it now," Tee said, and they both knew she was right.

Dad was never the same after that. Before long he had asked Mom for the divorce. From that point he went steadily downhill, eventually losing everything he owned.

Chapter Three
A Foretaste of Things to Come

The summer I graduated from eighth grade was the worst summer of my life. There was tremendous anger and bitterness between my parents now. Neither one came to my eighth-grade graduation because both assumed the other would be there, and they didn't want to see each other. For the same reason, they didn't come to see the end-of-school play I danced and acted in, nor were they there for a speech contest I won. During that time, it seemed I was always standing alone, while crowds of proud families swarmed around all my classmates.

Friends invited me to their homes for dinner, but I became painfully aware of what an oddity I was. Divorce was scandalous back then. Their parents quizzed me about what had happened, eager for intimate details. It was easier to just avoid everyone.

Iris and I stayed with Dad that summer, but everything was miserable and lonely. We all went our separate ways. Each morning I got up, packed myself a lunch, and took off on the back trails behind our house toward a secret hiding place I had found. It was a frightening walk for me. I had to cross a swamp where many years before a young girl had drowned in the quicksand. I imagined her terrified screams as I fearfully and gingerly made my way across the spongy ground.

The snakes I encountered were real, although small, but my vivid imagination conjured up oversized lizards and hungry alligators hiding among the tall, soggy grasses. On the other side of the swamp I followed a trail to a high railroad trestle. Every time I crossed it I worried about the sudden appearance of a train. At the end of the trestle lay the final barrier to my secret hideaway—a long curving tunnel. At the beginning and the end of the tunnel I could see where I was walking, but for a short distance in the very middle both ends were invisible, leaving me in smothering blackness. I kept one foot against a rail for that span of inky space, and it wasn't until I could see the light at the other end that I began to relax. I had almost reached my destination.

It was a rocky ledge that stretched out over the Willamette River, offering a calm and peaceful view of water and trees. I passed the time reading, eating my lunch, and thinking; sometimes sleeping in the warm sunshine, but always savoring the fact that I was out of sight of everyone.

I left my hiding place before dusk so I wouldn't have to cross the swamp in the darkness. When I walked into the house, if Dad was there, he'd always ask, "Did you have a good time today, Jeannie?"

"Yeah." I'd reply.

"What did you do?"

"Oh, I went down to the river."

"By yourself?"

"No." I lied. "I met some kids."

I was afraid Dad might forbid me to go if he knew I was alone. But actually, he was so wrapped up in his own misery that he probably wouldn't have cared.

Mom was too busy working to be much involved with Iris and me that summer. For the most part we were left to our own devices.

Iris began to hang out with a rough group of kids from the high school. I felt uncomfortable with them, so I didn't even have Iris for companionship. One evening, however, she invited me to go to a party with her. Desperate for company, I went. Everyone there was smoking and drinking, and Iris immediately joined in. Feeling very out of place, I went outside and sat down on the porch steps.

Soon a boy joined me. "Why'd you even come here if you're not going to join in the fun?" he demanded. "You make it hard on the rest of us by being such a little Puritan."

Without a word, I got up and walked away from the party. That summer I didn't seem to belong anywhere.

In early fall Iris and I moved to Portland, where Mom was managing an apartment house. We enrolled at Lincoln High School. It was a huge school in downtown Portland, far larger than any we had ever attended before, and as we walked to school that first morning in September, we were both very nervous.

There was a large, bronze statue of Abraham Lincoln just inside the double entry doors, and before separating we agreed to meet there for lunch. The minute the lunch bell rang, I ran to the statue, anxious to see how Iris had managed. Fifteen minutes later when she hadn't shown up, I began to worry. I wanted to go look for her, but was afraid she'd come while I was gone and think I had ditched her. Finally I sat down on some nearby steps to wait. She never came.

I went to my afternoon classes, but I was so worried about Iris I couldn't concentrate. After school I hurried back to the statue, hoping she'd be there. She wasn't. Again, I sat down to wait. Soon all the kids had gone home. Even the teachers left. Finally I gave up and headed home.

There I found Iris. The day had not gone well for her. She had found the immense horde of students far too intimidating, and halfway through the day she'd come home. She never went back to high school again.

After quitting school, Iris decided to enroll in beauty college. Dad wasn't giving Mom any financial support, and she was working long, arduous hours trying to make ends meet. To pay for Iris's tuition, she took an extra job as a supervisor of cosmetic sales, which meant she was gone two or three nights a week.

In spite of all our moving around, Roy Zeiler managed to keep track of me. He had a job as a Postal Telegraph boy and stopped by to see me whenever he was delivering telegrams in our vicinity.

One night we double-dated with Roy's brother and his girlfriend. Afterwards we drove the girlfriend home first. Before Roy's brother walked her to the door, he reached across the seat to kiss her. She met him halfway, and for long, endless minutes they continued to kiss. Roy and I sat mutely in the back seat, stiff as ramrods, flaming with embarrassment.

Finally Roy said, "Well..." and then he grabbed me and kissed me. I'd never really been kissed before and thought I would faint from lack of breath. I didn't realize it was possible to kiss and breathe at the same time; however, I caught on very quickly...and I *liked* it!

Meanwhile, Iris had begun dating a young man named Hall Burnham, and the four of us sometimes double-dated. None of us had much money, so Hall and Iris would buy themselves a ticket for a movie, then Hall would sneak Roy and me in the side door after the show had begun. We'd scurry up the stairs to the darkest corner of the balcony and congratulate ourselves for being so clever.

On the evenings Mom was out of town, Hall and Roy came to keep us company. One night Mom sat Iris, Hall, Roy, and me down for a chat. "If anything happens to you girls, everyone will blame *me* for giving you so much freedom. But I'm telling you right now that I trust all four of you." She paused and looked us each in the eye. "I'm putting you all on your honor. Don't let me down." We never did.

I hated how hard Mom had to work, and finally, after one term at Lincoln High School, I, too, dropped out. Because of my earlier training, I felt qualified to teach beginning tap dancing lessons and decided to open a studio in the basement of the apartments Mom managed. That would bring in some extra money and help with the bills. I charged fifty cents a lesson, and soon my studio was alive with little girls wanting to learn tap dancing and acrobatics. To keep ahead of my students, I took dancing lessons, too.

After awhile I held a recital to show off the girls' progress, and once a grade school invited my students to perform for their PTA meeting. We dazzled them with our intricate homemade costumes and decorations. I was doing what I loved, something that challenged my artistic ability. "Someday," I'd muse to myself as I demonstrated new steps for my students, "I'll be doing this on Broadway."

Just as my little studio was really building up, the apartment house Mom managed was sold. This not only meant another move; it meant closing my studio. By now, Mom, Iris, and I had become pros at survival. We could take the dingiest apartment or room and turn it into a cozy home; we could turn a scrap of fabric and a bit of lace into an evening gown. We knew how to live with a flair on the most meager income. We called ourselves "The Three Musketeers." Joining arms, we'd vow, "We'll sink or swim together."

One of our biggest challenges came when Mom took a job managing a rooming house for longshoremen. It was in a very rough part of town, near the waterfront. The streets were littered with homeless drunks and hopeless women. The men staying in the rooming house were a long way from their homes and families, if they even had any, so Mom did what she could to make the dingy place comfortable. She put up cheerful wallpaper, sewed bright slipcovers, and applied fresh paint to the woodwork. At Christmas she set up a large, festive tree and even managed to come up with a gift for each man on Christmas Eve, when everyone gathered together to celebrate.

Mom was admired by all the men, and they repaid her kindness by watching out for Iris and me. On Friday nights when we walked uptown to a movie, they stood unobtrusively on the street corners, making sure no harm came to us. One dark, rainy night a man reached out from a darkened doorway and grabbed Iris by the arm. Instantly, before she could even scream, one of the longshoremen materialized at her side and forced the man to release her. "Get home, girls!" he hissed...and we surely did!

Occasionally, Dad came to see Iris and me, but it was awkward for everyone. He always had a different woman with him, and although he didn't want us to know, he was now living in his old truck. He had lost everything—our home, the cars—everything. The memory of our once-happy family was fading in my mind. Sometimes it seemed as though I had made it all up.

Mom hated that I had quit school to teach dancing. At her insistence, after I lost my dancing studio, I agreed to go back to high school if I could graduate with the kids I had known at Oak Grove. By now they were more than a year ahead of me.

The fall of 1936 I entered Girls Polytechnic High School, determined to study very hard and catch up with my classmates. From the beginning, I loved this school. It wasn't nearly as overwhelming as Lincoln had been, and soon I had made many friends.

I joined the Thespian Drama Club and immediately got involved in the school plays. I also joined the Palette and Brush Club and won a couple of art and poster contests. I helped build stage sets and even wrote a Christmas program we performed with much gusto and success. I participated in these activities because it was what I loved. I didn't realize how valuable these versatile experiences would be later on in my life.

One afternoon at school, Dean Osborn and the Principal called me to the office. "Jean, there are two very important opportunities we'd like to talk to you about. You are qualified to run for either student body president or our school's Rose Festival Princess."

Their words filled me with pride. The Rose Festival was a celebration held every spring in Portland. It was the city's highlight of the year, attracting people from all over the country. Each high school elects one student to represent its school as a Rose Princess—something almost every girl dreamed of. Then, a queen was chosen from among the princesses to rule over the two-week -long celebration.

Dean Osborn interrupted my musings. "As you know, Jean, both positions are a tremendous honor, but you can't do both. Take some time to think over which position you'd like to run for."

After much consideration, I decided to aim for student body president, since I would hold that position for the entire year as opposed to the short time I would serve as a Rose Princess. Besides, I felt my limited wardrobe wasn't sufficient to meet the requirements of a Rose Princess. To my delight, when the ballots were counted two weeks later, I had won the student body presidency.

Walking down the hall after the election, I passed Rosie, a quiet, unobtrusive girl I had befriended. I smiled at her, expecting her congratulations. Instead, she walked by without speaking to me.

I caught her by the arm. "Rosie!" I exclaimed. "Why did you just ignore me?"

Her cheeks grew red, and she studied the toe of one shoe. "I figured you wouldn't want to be friends with me, now that you're student body president," she mumbled.

"Oh, Rosie! You're my friend! I don't want to be president if it means I'm going to lose my friends!"

Perhaps because I had seen how Iris suffered from the humiliation of being a "cripple," or maybe because the stigma of my parents' divorce had set me apart, I knew what it was like to be "different." My heart went out to anyone like Rosie, who had few friends or was teased by the other students.

I hated cruelty of any kind. For this reason, I refused an invitation to join our exclusive high school senior sorority.

"But why, Jean?" asked one of the leaders. "You're just the kind of girl we want to represent us."

"I think a sorority is a clique!" I told her honestly.

"Well, Jean," she replied, "You know we have to have some guidelines. We just can't let everyone in." I didn't agree and refused to become a member, to the chagrin of several girls.

Our home was always filled with "misfits" that I befriended. "Can't you ever bring home nice, 'normal' kids?" Mom asked me one afternoon.

"But, Mom," I countered, "nice, 'normal' kids don't need me."

With the exception of my English classes, I excelled at Girl's Polytechnic. I was determined to make up for the classes I had missed while I was running my dance studio, so I doubled up on required courses. It meant long hours of intense work and study, but the effort was worth it. My secret goal was to win a scholarship to Oregon State University.

When report cards were handed out at the end of the first grading period, I had received an A in every subject but English. Mrs. Foster had given me a C! Filled with dismay, I asked her why she had given me such a low grade.

"Jean, there is no way you can <u>honestly</u> get straight A's when taking as many subjects as you are. It can't be done."

"But I've completed all your assignments!" I countered. "I'm trying so hard for a scholarship...you know I don't deserve this C." She just folded her hands and looked at her desk. No matter how I pleaded, she refused to reconsider my grade.

The next term I didn't even try in Mrs. Foster's class. What was the point? However, when report cards were passed out that time I was flabbergasted to find she had given me a B. Again, I went to see her.

"Mrs. Foster," I said, holding out my report card, "I don't deserve this B any more than I deserved the C you gave me last term. I worked hard then; I did nothing special this term." I turned and left before she could respond.

From then on we were cool to each other, but I did complete all her assignments. Somehow, in spite of Mrs. Foster, I managed to win a full-tuition college scholarship, but that C still bothers me to this day.

The day our principal gave me the good news of the scholarship, I danced all the way home. "Mom! Mom!" I cried as I ran into our apartment waving the scholarship announcement in the air. "Look what I got!"

Mom read the announcement, and when she finally raised her eyes, she looked as if I had kicked her in the stomach.

"Am I supposed to support you all my life, Jean?" she asked bitterly. "You know your Dad doesn't help. This scholarship only pays for tuition. What about your room and board, your clothes? How can I manage that? You should never have applied."

Her words slammed against my heart, smashing all my joy. How could I have dared dream of something so impossible? Why had I worked so hard for something so out of reach?

The next day, heartsick, I went to the Dean's office to relinquish my scholarship.

"Jean, there must be some way..." Dean Osborn began, but I didn't let her finish.

"No, Ms. Osborn. There's not. I have to go to work." I left her office and walked down another long, lonely corridor.

As student body president, it was my responsibility to introduce our school's Rose Festival Princess to the city on the night of the Queen's Coronation. The Civic Auditorium was filled to capacity that night, and hundreds more, including my own mother, were turned away.

A few moments before I was to go out on stage, Commander Niles, my Rosarian escort, stepped on the hem of my full-length white organdy formal. The sound of tearing fabric froze us both in place.

"Good lord, Girl!" he exclaimed. "Something ripped! What have I done?" Looking down, we saw a narrow length of hem trailing us. Quickly swooping me up in his arms, he rushed me to a wardrobe seamstress in one of the dressing rooms. "I broke something!" he said abruptly to the startled woman as he set me down in front of her. "Please fix it. I'm so sorry!"

A few quick stitches and we were ready once again for our grand entrance. Knowing there was standing-room-only in the auditorium filled me with tremendous excitement. I had participated in several speech contests through school and acted in various plays, but never before such a large audience. Butterflies of anticipation fluttered in my stomach. *I could hardly wait.*

Commander Niles gallantly led me on stage to join the other student body presidents—all boys, all dressed in black suits. The princesses wore long, full-skirted, powder-blue gowns. Standing there in my white organdy formal, I couldn't decide if I looked like the main attraction or a misfit. I certainly stood out in the crowd.

Gliding over to my school's princess, I led her forward to the front of the vast stage. We gave a deep curtsy to the audience and then to each other. We had practiced this so many times, it was flawless. In response to my introduction of our Princess, the thunderous applause was an exhilarating song of acceptance to me. It carried me above the sadness that none of my family was in the audience to share this night with me. I memorized every detail of the evening so that I could re-enact it all for Mom and Iris when I got home. Truly, this was the greatest moment of my life thus far.

I was too excited to go straight home at the end of the evening. After the Coronation Ceremony I walked down Broadway in Portland. The city was mine that night as I swept along in my beautiful gown. My borrowed cape and the lovely corsage that Commander Niles had carefully pinned on my shoulder made me feel like a queen, indeed. How appropriate that the main street in downtown Portland was called Broadway. Three thousand miles to the East, in New York City, was another glittering street by the same name. Someday I would walk down that one, too.

Shortly thereafter came my graduation. I had worked hard for this, and on the night of the Commencement Services I arrived at the school full of a satisfying sense of achievement. The only damper on my happiness was the fact that once again Mom and Dad were both absent. Four years had passed since the divorce, but time had done nothing to lessen their bitterness. They still went to great lengths to avoid each other, and both had assumed that the other would be attending my graduation.

But for once, I was not alone. Roy Zeiler had come and brought a carload of friends from Oak Grove with him. He looked very handsome that night in his dress slacks and jacket. The Adam's apple that had once been so prominent on his skinny neck was beginning to disappear, and his long, gangly body was taking on the attractive physique of a man. Admiring him now, I wondered if there would come a time when our friendship would evolve into something more. He'd been my buddy since fifth grade. What would happen now that our school years were over?

I gave my farewell speech to the student body, accepted my diploma from the Dean, and walked away from Girls Polytechnic for the last time. That night, before going to sleep, I knelt by the window in our bedroom. Gazing up at the stars, I contemplated my future. While it was true that college was no longer possible, there were still many dreams to pursue. There had to be a path for me. I would let nothing stand in my way.

Chapter Four
Trying My Wings

My first job after graduation was selling magazines in the state of Washington. My assigned selling area was a logging operation. Few of the men could either read or write. Undaunted, I showed them LOOK magazine, with more pictures than words. They smiled and eagerly signed an "x" where I told them to. I was so successful, my boss assigned me to the waterfront in Everett, Washington, where I was to sell magazines to the Japanese fishing fleet. She figured if I could sell magazines to loggers and some men who couldn't read, I could sell them to foreigners who didn't speak English.

After one or two attempts, however, I refused to go down there alone. The waterfront was a dark, sinister place with scary men lurking in the shadows. Few people on the boats I approached spoke English. I was naive, but not so much so that I couldn't see this was not a place for a young girl to be working alone. I could disappear completely. When I asked the sales manager to change my selling location or send someone with me, she refused. Although I was making good money, it was not worth the danger I faced each day. There seemed no option but to quit.

"So, Jean," smirked my boss when I told her. "What are you going to do now? Go home and wash baby bottoms all your life?"

I fled from her office and her stinging remarks. Throwing my clothes into a suitcase, I climbed on a bus for Portland and cried all the way home.

"I'm a failure!" I wept into my mother's arms. "I'm doomed to mess up. I've failed at my very first job!"

Mom patted my head soothingly, saying all the right things to me.

"You're not a failure, Jeannie." She hugged me tight. "Your boss should never have assigned such an area to you.

You'll be a great success one day—just you wait and see. I've never doubted it for a minute."

After that experience, I decided to stick with what I knew best—dancing. Lying about my age, I joined a traveling dance troupe that performed in nightclubs around northern California. I thrived, once again doing what I loved, and in the process, made good money.

When the night club tour ended, we all came back to Portland to regroup. Once again at home with Mom and Iris in our small apartment, I got a chance to dance for a two-week stand at a nightclub in Longview, Washington. My salary would be twenty-five dollars a week less a ten percent commission for my agent. To me, it sounded like a fortune, and I was thrilled.

The show was to close on Christmas Eve, and I discovered that I could catch an express bus back to Portland at 1:00 a.m. Christmas morning. I sent a telegram to Mom to let her know I was coming.

"MERRY CHRISTMAS EVERYTHING UNDER CONTROL BE HOME TOMORROW 2 A.M."

That night the club manager let me do my last show a little early so I wouldn't miss the bus. He even gave me my $50.00 in earnings in advance. When the show ended, there wasn't enough time to even take off my heavy stage makeup. I threw a dress and coat on over my costume and ran out the door. I made it to the depot just in the nick of time, huffing and puffing as I bought my ticket and boarded the Greyhound bus.

When we pulled into the Portland terminal I hailed a cab to take me to Mom's. The cab driver glowered at me in disapproval. He took one look at my heavy makeup and suitcase and concluded that I was a "woman of the streets." He was quite rude. I tried to explain the situation, but all he said was, "Yeah, yeah...sure." After that I sat still as a mouse all the way uptown.

When we arrived at the apartment where Mom and Iris lived, he asked what number to ring. He pressed the button, obviously expecting a man's voice to answer. Instead, he

Jean doing acrobatic dancing

was startled by Mom's gentle voice. "Hi, Jeannie! Iris and I are waiting."

The cab driver looked as if someone had clubbed him as he passed the receiver to me. "Hi, Mom!" I said. "I made it!" The buzzer clicked to unlock the door, and the cab driver, his attitude suddenly warm, held it open for me. He even offered to help with my suitcase, although he'd let me drag it out of the cab and up to the door by myself. I thanked him and even gave him a tip, feeling relieved to be redeemed in his eyes.

I flew down the hall to where Mom and Iris waited by our door. We all hugged and then sat down on the bed. Earlier, I had asked for my fifty-dollar wages to be paid in small bills. Now I took them out of my purse and gleefully showered them all over Mom and Iris. It looked like a million dollars, and we all laughed and hugged again. We felt so rich! What a Christmas we three had together—"The Three Musketeers."

In 1940, Iris married Hall Burnham, the young man she had been dating for some time. The marriage turned into a nightmare for her when Hall began drinking heavily. He was gone far more hours than his work required, leaving Iris home alone for long periods of time. Although Mom had paid for her to go to beauty college, Iris never put her training to use. Instead, she sat in their apartment and fretted about Hall's absences, and his accusations when he was home.

One evening she called me, frantic. "Hall never came home from work," she wept. "I don't know what I should do."

I took the bus over to see her. I had been there about an hour when Hall stumbled through the door, roaring drunk. Iris took one look at him and fled to the kitchen.

"Where's the guy?" growled Hall. "I know you've got a guy here..."

"Hall, please..." whimpered Iris. "There's no one here but Jean."

Without a word he drew back his hand and slapped Iris hard across the face, sending her reeling against the kitchen table. Seething with rage, but hesitant to interfere, I picked up my coat to leave.

Hall blocked my way. "Stay and watch the fun," he said.

I looked at him in contempt. "You're worthless, Hall. Let me by."

Again his hand swung out. The back of it caught my face, its force flinging me against the wall. My head shattered a mirror as I crumpled to the floor, momentarily stunned. Blood trickled from a cut on my mouth. For several seconds I stared at Hall, utterly dumbfounded.

Cold as ice, I pulled myself up off the floor and lunged at him, fueled by a fury I'd never felt before. Catching him off guard, I stomped my high-heeled pump into his foot, at the same time dragging my fingernails down both his cheeks. They left a gratifying trail of blood. Then, picking up my coat, I stalked passed him. Hall stood frozen in stunned silence, all the fight gone out of him. He had never had a woman fight back before. As the door closed behind me, I could hear Iris's muffled weeping.

Outside I broke into a run toward the nearest bus stop. I was stumbling up the steps of the bus before I realized I didn't have enough money for the fare. The astonished driver took one look at my bruised, bleeding face and let me on anyway.

"Are you all right?" he asked. I nodded and slumped onto the side seat.

Twenty minutes later I was at Mom's, shivering as I related what had happened. "Mom, I could have killed him," I said. "I could have done it easily." I felt certain of it.

Two months later Iris called, begging me to come for dinner. She said Hall wanted to talk to me. I refused. I had no desire to ever see or speak to him again. Iris continued to plead with me, until, for her sake, I finally agreed. Hanging up, I wondered if I would ever stop trying to make life easier for her.

Taking the bus across town, I found Hall waiting at the bus stop when I got off. The minute I looked at him, deep loathing flooded through me.

"Where's Iris?" I asked sharply.

"She didn't come."

I turned to walk away, but he clutched my arm. "Please Jean, I've got to talk to you...I'm sorry about what happened."

I looked him squarely in the eyes. "I wouldn't be here at all except for Iris. If you ever touch me again, Hall, I'll crawl across the world on my belly, if need be, until I find you, and then I'll kill you." I spoke with quiet certainty. Then I turned and walked away. Forgive Hall was one thing I could not do— not even for Iris.

Their marriage would not last. It was stormy and hateful from the beginning, and we were all relieved when it ended in divorce. It was a blessing that Iris survived and that no children were born from that union.

Several years later I bumped into Hall on the streets of Portland. Weak, lonely, and old before his time, he smiled sadly at me. I had heard a rumor that he had terminal cancer. Seeing him, I knew it must be true. Somehow, I couldn't hate him anymore.

"Hello, Jean." He looked wistfully at me.

I nodded. "Hall..." It was all I could say. To see him this way, to remember the good days when he was courting Iris and the happiness we all thought would last forever...then to think about the wasted life now standing so frail and gaunt before me, was so very sad. There was nothing more to say, so we finally just walked on past each other. Hall died that winter.

About the time that Hall and Iris began having marital trouble, I got a job teaching ballroom dancing for the Oregon Institute of Dancing in downtown Portland. I became good friends with Dave and Birdie, the owners of the Institute, and one weekend they invited me to go fishing with them. Dave had just bought a brand new Buick, and he and Birdie wanted to try it out by driving to Detroit, Oregon, about seventy miles southeast of Portland. Dave's friend, Jim, was also going, and they wanted me to make it a foursome.

We left Portland at 3:00 a.m. in order to reach our destination before sunrise. A dam was being built on the Santiam River just below Detroit, and the tortuous mountain road was under construction. It was covered with a thick layer of gravel, forcing Dave to go slower and slower. As we came around one very sharp curve, the gravel sucked at the wheels drawing us toward a two-hundred-foot drop-off. As if in slow motion, the front of the car slid off the road and began a sickening somersault over the cliff's edge.

Inside the car, time seemed to stand still as our bodies were hurled about. Then, with a sickening jolt, the car came to an abrupt stop upside down. Birdie's screams tore through the approaching dawn as I struggled to gather my wits. A fierce pressure pushed against the middle of my back as I became aware of a crushing weight on top of me. Looking around, I realized I was lying on the inside roof of the car. The seat was holding me down, and Jim was slung over the top of the seat. The dome light felt as though it were imbedded in my back.

Gritting my teeth against the pain and pressure gouging my spine, I inched my way from under the seat. The rear window had been knocked out, and I crawled toward it. Unable to comprehend the precarious position of the car, I could only think of one thing: getting out to find help.

The next thing I knew I was falling through the window and tumbling further down the steep slope. Frantically I clawed at bushes, trying to break my fall, and finally managed to grab one. I swallowed the scream of pain that rose in my throat as my body jerked to a halt. Gasping for air, I looked up from where I had stopped and shuddered. Twenty feet directly above me, Dave's new Buick rested lengthwise and upside down on a tree trunk growing horizontally out of the steep mountainside.

Clawing my way back up the cliff, I finally reached the road just as the first light of dawn pierced the darkness. Not knowing which way to go, I started walking up the heavily graveled road. Headlights appeared ahead, and I raised my arms to flag them down. As the lights drew near, all feeling suddenly left my body, and I pitched forward on my face.

Miraculously, Dave, Birdie, and Jim were not seriously injured in the accident, but I had a crushed vertebra. The doctors wrapped my battered torso in stiff, castlike bandages and told me I would never dance again. I refused to believe them. My dreams were wrapped up in my ability to dance. I had to prove them wrong.

When I was released from the hospital a week later, I went straight to the dance studio. Dave sat me in a chair, my body still swathed in one big, stiffened bandage, and I watched the students dancing.

"Dave, I want to try to dance."

"Oh, Jean, no! You can't do that..."

"Help me stand, Dave. I want to try."

Reluctantly, he lifted me to my feet and placed his hands at my waist. I took one small, slow step. *It felt good!* I took another. *Even better!* Painstakingly, we made our way around the edge of the dance floor until Dave finally convinced me to go home and rest.

I returned to the dance studio the very next morning and every day after, determined to keep dancing. Soon I convinced Dave to let me resume teaching, even though I was still hampered by bandages. By now he knew I could not be stopped, so he assigned me some beginning students.

The bandages stayed on for several more weeks. When they were finally removed, huge patches of my skin came off with them. In place of the bandages I now had oozing scabs, but at least I could move more freely. Ignoring the pain, I immediately started to work on my dance routines, while my doctors shook their heads in dismay, and then resignation. They just did not understand that I *had to dance*. I truly believe that dancing helped my healing and total recovery more than anything else.

Not long after my accident, Mom began going to Saturday night dances held around Portland. Sometimes I joined her there after work. We liked the Cotillion Dance Hall the best. A man by the name of Ben Hersey liked to go there also, and he began to dance a lot with Mom. I could see little sparks fly whenever they waltzed off together. Mom asked him to our apartment for dinner a time or two, and within a few months they were quietly married. Mom moved to Ben's home near Beaverton, Oregon, and I got a smaller apartment by myself.

Soon thereafter, my world was once again shattered. Only this time, it wasn't just *my* world—it was everyone's.

It was a chilly December afternoon, and I was in my tiny kitchen, when I heard a strange crackling on the radio followed by a voice shaking with emotion. *"We interrupt this program to inform you that the Japanese have just bombed Pearl Harbor..."* The bowl I was holding fell from my hands and shattered at my feet as I stood there, stunned. It felt as if the earth had just shifted on its axis, unbalancing everything as I knew it. It would be many years before that feeling completely left me.

That evening at 7:00, Americans all across the country hovered around their radios to hear President Roosevelt's address. His words chilled me to the bone: "...*Since the premeditated attack on Pearl Harbor on December 7, 1941, a state of war exists between the United States and the Empire of Japan...*"

Immediately men flooded the Armed Services recruiting offices to sign up for active duty, including my childhood friend, Roy Zeiler. Roy tried to join the Navy, but was stamped Army 4-F because of impaired vision in one eye, the result of a childhood accident. This meant he would stay stateside. He was to be sworn into the Army in three weeks. If he could board some ship before his induction he could go overseas—something he was desperate to do. He went down to the Sailor's Union of the Pacific Hiring Hall, but all the positions were filled. Refusing to give up, he continued to haunt the Merchant Seamen's Hall. Just when it was looking hopeless, word came that a man had jumped ship. Roy was offered his place as the assistant to the ship's carpenter. Not until the ship actually pulled away from the dock, headed toward the high seas, did he breathe easily. Only then was he sure he was at last on his way.

I hadn't seen him in a long time, but when a friend told me that Roy had gone overseas with the Merchant Marines I wasn't surprised. Roy would have done anything to serve his country. Still, I worried. What would happen to him? Would I ever see him again?

It was a very emotional, unsettled time. All around me friends were getting caught up in wartime romances. Mom and Iris were both married now, and Dad was stumbling around in his own darkness. I felt very unconnected.

One day at the Oregon Institute of Dancing a tall, charismatic young man came in for lessons. I was quite flattered by his lavish attentions, and before long we were married. Not long afterwards he was shipped overseas, and it was a long time before we saw each other again. When we did, we were total strangers. As much as I had hated my parents' divorce, I found myself following in their footsteps as my brief marriage came to an end.

Not long afterwards, Dave, the owner of the Oregon Institute of Dancing, died of a heart attack, and his wife sold the studio. So, like thousands of other Americans, I got involved in the war effort. I took a war training course where I studied blueprint drawing, riveting, drilling, and sheet metal and tool design.

In May of 1942 I went to work for Columbia Aircraft in their Inspection Department, doing magnetic tests and inspections of parts for PBY tail assemblies and bomb bay doors for Douglas Bombers. As I completed each inspection, I stamped the part with my #7 stamp. I referred to it as my "lucky seven," hoping it would bring good fortune to the crew. I couldn't help but wonder about the fate of these parts and planes. *How many would make it safely back home?*

In the evenings I took a drafting course. I loved the challenge drafting offered, and it soon became apparent that I had a natural aptitude for it. When my boss at Columbia Aircraft discovered my drafting skills, he began having me sketch parts as well as continue with my other responsibilities. I didn't get paid for my drafting, but he did promise to have me transferred to that section, where I really wanted to work. However, weeks went by with no sign that a transfer was forthcoming.

One day I confronted him. "Mr. Butterfield, you keep promising me a transfer to the drafting and engineering department, but it never seems to come through."

"Well, Jean," he said blandly, "I'd love to help you, but all our positions are "frozen" right now, including yours. There's a war going on, you know. I can't do anything about it."

"Well, I can!" I assured him. "I can quit!"

"You'd better have another job to go to before you do," he said. His tone implied it wasn't likely I would get another job anytime soon. It was just the challenge I needed.

On my next lunch hour I went across town to a factory that made balsa-wood life rafts for the Navy. A short time later I walked out of Air King Life Raft Company with a job. On my way back to Columbia Aircraft, I stopped at a florist and bought a large white calla lily, such as people send to funerals, and a sympathy card. At work, I took the flower and card down to the mail room and asked them to deliver it to Mr. Butterfield. It traveled through three buildings before it reached him, gathering curious stares and questions from everyone along the way.

I hadn't been at my desk very long before he called me into his office. "Jean, what is the meaning of this?" he asked gruffly, as he gestured toward the lily and held up the card.

"It means I'm leaving," I explained calmly. "You told me to find another job before I quit, so I did!"

"But Jean, I didn't think you'd take me seriously! You put me on the spot..."

"You put *me* on the spot," I countered.

Mr. Butterfield shook his head in regret. "You've been a good employee, Jean. I'm sorry to lose you."

While working for Air King Life Raft Company, I still continued with my evening drafting course. One night, a man came in to observe our work. He walked all around the room, then came and stood by my drafting table. After watching me draw for several minutes, he asked, "Are you wanting a job?"

"Oh, no," I replied flippantly. "I'm just doing this for the fun of it." I didn't really think he was serious.

He shrugged. "If you do want a job, come see me." After he walked away, I noticed he had left his business card on the corner of my drafting table. I took it to my instructor.

"Who is this?" I asked him.

He looked at the name. "Tom Taylor? He's a real comer among the architects and engineers here in Portland."

"Well, he just offered me a job!" I grinned.

"Jean!" he exclaimed. "I suggest you go see him!"

The next day, I did just that. Putting on my new tailored suit, I swept my hair up on top of my head for a more mature, professional look. Gathering my purse and gloves, I went to his office.

Opening the door, I saw Mr. Taylor bent over a set of drawings on a drafting table. "I've come to see about a job," I announced.

Tom Taylor looked at me over the top of his glasses. "As a secretary?" he queried.

I realized he didn't recognize me as the young girl in pigtails and blue jeans he had given his card to in the drafting class the night before.

"No, as a draftsman. You talked to me in class."

"*You're the girl in pigtails?*" he asked in astonishment.

I smiled and nodded, feeling quite foolish.

"You're hired!" he grinned. "Can you start right now?"

That was the beginning of a long and successful working relationship with Tom Taylor. I worked with him three different times during my life, and many years later at his retirement banquet, where I was asked to speak on behalf of his engineering staff, I joked that the only way Tom could get rid of me was to retire himself.

I stayed with Tom Taylor during most of the war years until I was offered a very special job in Santa Ana, California, drafting underground fueling systems for the Post Engineers at the Santa Ana Army Air Base. Tom agreed it was too good an opportunity to turn down, so I packed my bags for a new adventure.

"I'll see you when the war is over," I told him on my last day of work.

He smiled. "I'll take that as a promise."

It didn't take long to settle into my small studio apartment in Santa Ana. It had a minute Pullman kitchen and bath, and a Murphy bed that folded down from a wall. I relished the warm California climate and the palm trees—so different from the lush but damp Portland area.

I enjoyed my new job and being part of the war effort. As full of uncertainties as the war years were, it was also a very patriotic time. We had immense pride in our country and in the men risking their lives for it. Everyone worked together to keep our spirits high.

One day during my lunch hour, I walked out across the airstrip to look at a graveyard of old planes no longer airworthy. Rusted, dented, some bearing blasts and bullet scars from aerial combat, they looked as forlorn as the forgotten residents of an old-folks home, their days of glory forever gone.

Walking along row after row of planes, I ran my hand across some of the faded, peeling flag decals that represented enemy planes shot down. Far off to one side of the field, I caught a glimpse of an old Douglas Bomber. Winding my way through the metal corpses to get a closer look, I could see it had been badly damaged; one wheel was missing. However, its fuselage was covered with a glory of flag decals—mute testimony to all its missions and all the young men who had flown with it.

Curiosity sent me to my knees, and I crawled underneath the belly of that old, dead plane. Craning my neck, I looked up at the bomb bay doors. There I found a faint, but very definite #7. My inspection stamp! This was one of *my* planes!

"Oh, you made it!" I cried, bursting into tears as I hunched beneath the carcass and caressed the dented metal around the #7. "You made it all the way home!"

As I crawled back out from underneath, my tears continued to flow. Now I knew that at least one of my planes had made it home. I felt as if I had flown every single mission with that old bomber.

About that same time, I got involved with the Community Theater in Santa Ana. One of the plays I performed in was "Junior Miss," where I played the second lead, Fuffy Adams.

An anonymous admirer sent my name in for an acting scholarship to play Summer Stock at Priscilla Beach Playhouse on Cape Cod, and I won it. With no more fanfare than that, the dream I had been nurturing throughout my life suddenly slid into focus. I didn't even think about it. After I received the notification in the mail, I called my boss at the air base and told him about winning the scholarship. He was elated for me and arranged for another draftsman to take over my job. The timing was perfect for my departure, as I had just completed the drawings needed to finalize the special fueling systems. I spent the rest of the day packing up my things to ship home to Oregon. Tomorrow I was eastward bound.

Jean sitting on the floor in a formal gown

Chapter Five
Heading East

The bus trip to the East Coast took three days and four nights in the middle of a sweltering June. The monotonous miles crawled by. I passed the time imagining what the future held. How glorious to be heading straight for my heart's desire! My aim was set for nothing short of acting on Broadway in New York City.

I promised myself I would do three things when I reached New York:

1. I'd find Times Square and kiss it.
2. I'd buy myself a hat on 5th Avenue.
3. On my opening night on Broadway, I would take a carriage ride through Central Park. (It couldn't be just any carriage. It had to be round-shaped, like Cinderella's carriage, be pulled by a white horse, and the driver would have to be wearing a top hat.) There was not the slightest doubt in my mind that all of this would happen. The only question was, when?

I got off the bus in Boston and took another to Plymouth, Massachusetts. From there I called the Theater Colony to be picked up. While waiting for my ride, I decided to visit Plymouth Rock. It turned out to be one of my greatest disappointments on the East Coast. Since the Pilgrims had landed there, I had assumed it was a very large rock—something like the Rock of Gibraltar that they saw from a distance while still on their ship. What a surprise to find it to be very, very small; so small that a cupola had even been built over it, as if it needed protection. How the Pilgrims had located such a small rock was beyond me!

I did not have long to ponder my disappointment, because my ride to Priscilla Beach arrived. As my final destination drew near, I became quite nervous. This was a whole new world I was walking into; nothing was familiar here, nothing secure.

After being assigned a small sleeping room in one of the colony houses, I was shown around the grounds and given time to unpack. Auditions before the faculty and directors were being held the next morning. I hardly slept at all that night because of my excitement and anticipation.

My alarm was set to go off early so I would have plenty of time to get ready for the auditions. I wanted to be as calm as possible. Before leaving for the theater, I gave my hair a final pat, smoothed my dress, and walked out of the room. A sense of destiny seemed to echo all around me.

Inside the theater it took a few minutes for my eyes to adjust to the dim lighting. Gradually I saw a panel of several directors and coaches sitting towards the center front near the stage. I took a seat on the side aisle among the other eager auditioners. It was briefly explained to us that we would be called one by one to perform a previously memorized poem or monologue of our own choosing. We would be graded from the moment we left our seat until we sat back down, even on whether or not we looked at the steps as we climbed them to the stage.

I soon discovered the directors and coaches were not there to coddle us. They appeared to have no concern whatsoever for the feelings of the fledgling actors. Sitting there listening as others were called before me, I was shocked by the cutting remarks.

"You're wasting our time!" they snarled at one beautiful blonde girl from the South. "Go back to Georgia and lose that drawl before you come back here."

One young man was interrupted barely into his monologue. "Don't bother finishing!"

The biggest disadvantage for the auditioners seemed to be their accents. I was thankful to be from the west coast, a melting pot where all accents are somewhat blended together.

By the time my name was called, my confidence was in great jeopardy. Somehow I managed to walk up the steps (without looking down) and over to center stage. Taking a deep breath

I launched into my chosen monologue. As soon as the first words left my mouth, my innate confidence returned. I loved performing more than anything else in the world. The directors were a tougher audience than usual, but they were still an audience. I determined to please them.

"Stop!" The command startled me in mid-sentence. I had thought everything was going very well. "Go sit over there," barked one of the coaches, pointing to the side of the auditorium.

Bewildered, I left the stage. *Now what?* I wondered, not knowing whether to laugh or cry.

When auditions were finished, one of the coaches came over and assigned me to a director. I looked at him in confusion, still not knowing what was going on.

"You got a part!" he explained, as if I were somewhat dimwitted. "A lead! Congratulations!" He winked at me.

Stunned and thrilled, I was given my script, and immediately I went to work memorizing the part of Jane in the play "Nine Girls." I wanted to have the words of the first act down pat before the first rehearsal. I didn't realize what a mistake that was. I soon learned that words and actions must be memorized together, not separately. I had the part down word perfect, but it didn't make sense to me and the more I practiced the more mechanical my lines sounded. Even after I added the actions I still couldn't make the part come alive. Frantic, unable to sleep from worry, I rehearsed my lines again and again until I was nearly incoherent with exhaustion, but I still could not sleep.

One night, as I perched on the edge of a couch saying some of my lines, I fell asleep, only to wake up a few minutes later, sobbing because of the time I had wasted. Dragging myself back to my sleeping room, I flopped down across the bed and fell into an exhausted sleep. Three hours later I woke up, once again crying. It was five a.m. Rehearsal was to begin at eight.

I decided to take a walk to clear my mind. Dawn was just starting to lighten the eastern sky and the air blew clean, refreshing my mind. Taking a deep breath I started through my lines again, only this time I pretended my sister Iris was there with me, and I spoke the words to her. It was the trick I needed. The part came alive. *Suddenly I was Jane!*

There is a way of acting called the Stanislavski Method, which instructs actors to "live the part." Stanislavski was a Russian director who gained great fame for his realistic portrayal of characters. He taught his actors to study the inner lives of characters as if they were real people and to "live the part" even when they were not acting.

While it is a very effective way of acting, it is also possible for an actor to become drawn so far into his character that he loses his own identity. I was so bent on playing Jane to perfection that I completely became the timid, mousy character— the exact opposite of my own flamboyant personality. Halfway through rehearsals of my second play, I realized I was still Jane. I could not seem to shake her off. This had a drastic effect on my acting. The director was aware of what was happening and was considering not casting me again in another play. I knew I was losing my edge.

Frantic, I began taking long walks, hoping the fresh sea breeze would blow away Jane. Although I was not a Christian, I even prayed for God's help. Gradually, the character of Jane began to recede, and my own personality finally re-emerged; but it never occurred to me to thank God. After that I was very careful to not let myself get drawn so far into any part.

On June 6, 1944, we were told the Allies were invading Normandy. Bells began to ring all around the Theater Colony. About midnight, I walked over to the theater, for me the nearest thing to a church. I believed in God and sometimes prayed, but I did not know it was possible to have a personal relationship with Him. Inside the theater I walked down to the front rows and, in the dim light, prayed for the servicemen involved in this invasion.

I had heard nothing about Roy Zeiler since the war began. *Was he a part of the invasion?* I wondered. *Was he even still alive?* So many lives had been lost already; everyone had been touched by death in some way.

Soon, several other members of the colony drifted in and sat quietly in the stillness of the little theater. The night air continued to carry the sounds of distant bells and sirens as the people in town celebrated the invasion of Normandy. Sometimes it seemed as if we had been at war forever. We all hoped this would be the catalyst to bring it to an end.

Franklin Trask, who owned Priscilla Beach Playhouse, also owned Boston Stock Company that played at Brattle Hall in Cambridge, Massachusetts. He said if I would come play Winter Stock for the full season, he would help me become a member in the Actor's Equity Association. In order to get a part in a Broadway play you had to belong to the Actor's Union. Few theater companies hired nonunion actors. Having heard how difficult it was for beginners to advance to union status, I eagerly accepted Trask's offer.

Brattle Hall was a wonderful old building, steeped in early American history. Compelling arguments for America's independence were given within its walls by men like Paul Revere and Patrick Henry. History had been planned and made here. Standing alone inside those musty walls, I could almost hear the ancient echoes of patriots' voices as they planned the Boston Tea Party. It seemed a great honor to be given the chance to mix my voice with all the other voices that had been heard in Brattle Hall.

Performing in older theaters like this one made me very grateful for the training I had received from Doris Smith, the director of Civic Theater in Portland, Oregon. She taught me to project my voice and enunciate my words by placing a small piece of wooden matchstick between my top and bottom front teeth and speaking around it. This forced my voice to the front of my mouth, exaggerating the lip movements. As a result my voice rang loud and clear even when the acoustics were not the best.

A play performed that winter at Brattle Hall was "Pursuit of Happiness." One of the parts was that of a seductive little Spanish waitress named Meg. It was such a spicy role that everyone clamored for it. I didn't think I had a chance to get such a coveted part, but I won it hands down. Afterwards I asked the director why he had cast me as Meg over everyone else.

"I'll tell you, Jeannie," he said, "but I'm not sure if you'll take it as a compliment or an insult. Over the years I have learned never to give the part of a trollop to a trollop. You give it to a saint—someone as pure as the driven snow—because she will play the part with great abandon, just the way she imagines a trollop to be."

I took it as a compliment. If my "saintly" persona was what got me the part, so be it.

It was while doing Winter Stock in Boston that I received my first fan letter. In part, it read:

> *"Dear Miss Lovelace,*
>
> *I want to compliment you on your marvelous characterization of Annabelle last night. I was watching you particularly, and I certainly enjoyed every minute you were on stage. If you continue to do as well, I'll be saying 'I knew her when'..!*
>
> *Sincerely,*
>
> *M. K. Bassett"*

Her words delighted me, making me feel like a legitimate actress now that I had a fan letter. However, Winter Stock was soon going to be over, and Mr. Trask had yet to do anything to get me into the Actor's Equity Association. Without that membership, my career as an actress would be severely hampered, and my dream of acting in a Broadway play impossible. One afternoon I approached him about it.

"Well, Jean," he replied after listening to me, "if I sign you into the Union, I'll have to pay you full salary. I can't afford to do that—especially when you're not playing leads."

"But Mr. Trask! You *promised* me I'd be union by the time the season ends, and it's almost over now!"

"Sorry, Jean," he said, with no regret whatsoever in his voice. "I can't afford it just now—maybe next year..."

I realized he had never intended to get me into the Actor's Union. Understanding this now, I drew myself slowly out of my chair so that I was looking down at him where he sat behind his impressive desk.

"I will never work for you again!" I said enunciating each word distinctly, and in one of my best dramatic exits, I whirled around and swooped out of his office.

Back in my room, despair draped itself around my shoulders. *How could I become the actress I wanted to be without Union status? I understood that the first thing every casting director asked for was an Actor's Equity card.* From then on my lack of a card became a noose around my neck. I would not breathe easy until I found some way to get into the Union.

Squaring my shoulders, I stared at myself in the mirror. *Who needs Mr. Trask?* I asked my reflection. *I will find another way to get into the Union.*

I grabbed my suitcase from the closet and laid it open across the bed. *Now's as good a time as any to head for New York!* I decided. With my few belongings packed I headed for the train depot. Maybe I was wrong to quit Franklin Trask, but...

Inside the Boston depot, I found a bench off to one side, away from the crush of people. As I waited for my train's departure, I stared down at my ticket. "DESTINATION: GRAND CENTRAL STATION, NYC" proclaimed the bold letters. Until now, I had only seen this ticket in my imagination. Now it was a tangible piece of paper—no longer a dream! A shiver of anticipation raced through me.

I knew that the road to Broadway would take a lot of hard work. That didn't scare me. But I also knew it would take some luck, and that made me nervous. I did not know how to make luck happen.

Once on the train, reality set in. I had no plans beyond this point. Turning toward the window, I saw my reflection and came face to face with what I *really* was—a small town girl a long way from home who knew no one, had no place to live, and no place to work.

Just what do you intend to do next? I prodded myself as I watched the countryside slide past my window. It was time to put feet to my dreams. New York was only minutes away!

By the time the train pulled into Grand Central Station, I had formulated a loose plan. Having heard other actors talk about the Empire Hotel near the Theater District in New York City, I decided to get a room there for the night. Then I would call my sister's friend, Helen Green, who was a dancer with the New York Civic Opera. She and Iris had always kept in touch, and she had told Iris to have me look her up if I ever made it to New York. As vague as it was, it felt good having a "plan."

Getting off the train, I lugged my suitcase through the milling crowds of people inside Grand Central Station. At last outside, the noise of the immense hordes of traffic and people muffled my thoughts as I stood transfixed by my first glimpse of this massive city. Portland, the largest city in Oregon, was a country village compared to this huge, teeming metropolis.

My adrenaline pounded in response to the city as I walked toward the string of taxis stretching along the curb. Choosing one at random, I gave the driver the address of the Empire Hotel and climbed into the back seat. *I was really in New York City!*

The Empire was a stately, middle-to-upper-class hotel with taxi stands in front and a uniformed doorman assisting guests into the lobby. Plush carpeted floors and tiled entries into various offices led the way to the impressive registration desk. Feeling hopelessly lost, but pretending to be right at home, I sauntered up to the desk. I asked for a room, stifling a gasp when told the price. Other arrangements would have to be found immediately, but for tonight this was it.

Settled in my room, I looked Helen's name up in the phone book, sure she'd be able to help. Maybe I could even stay with her until I found a place of my own. Unfortunately, when I dialed her number, the building manager informed me Helen was out of town for two weeks. My hand trembled as I slowly replaced the receiver. Now I <u>was</u> alone! My "plan" didn't reach beyond this point.

Sitting on the bed, I looked around the room, and panic welled up inside. *Okay, Jeannie,* I told myself sternly. *You can sit here and mope, or you can get on with it. What's it gonna be?*

In answer, I stood up, smoothed my dress, ran a brush through my hair and left the room. This was the time to make good on one of the three promises I had made myself concerning New York City. Downstairs in the lobby, I asked the concierge for directions to Times Square and marched resolutely out the door. The gentleman seemed to think I was important—and so I was!

Times Square turned out to be as big a surprise as Plymouth Rock. I had imagined there would be an actual square or monument—something <u>kissable</u>. Instead, it was just a large multi-cornered intersection of streets. My eyes searched around for something to kiss, but found nothing. Still, a promise is a promise. I looked to be sure no one was watching me, kissed the tips of my fingers, then stooped down and brushed them on the sidewalk.

I stood up, exhilaration seeping from every pore. I had made it to New York City. I had kissed Times Square. *Get ready Broadway,* I whispered, *here I come!*

I was about to board a street car to take me back up Broadway to the Empire when I noticed a blind man also waiting to board. I spoke to him and offered my arm to help him up the steps, then guided him to a double seat where we both sat down. I felt I had done my good deed for the day.

"You're in show business, aren't you?" he asked after we were seated.

"Why, yes!" I answered in surprise. "How did you know?"

He told me he had been a scriptwriter for Paramount Studios for many years and could tell by my voice. "You've had training," he explained. "You speak like an actress."

Wow! I thought, *It shows. Even a blind man can tell I'm an actress!*

He asked where I was staying, and I told him I had just arrived and needed to find less expensive quarters.

"There's a small residential hotel over on West 81st, near my place," he said. "Why don't you ride uptown with me, and I'll take you to it?"

I wasn't sure if I should accompany a strange man to a hotel or not, but since he was blind, I reasoned I could outrun him if it became necessary. We went to the hotel, and he introduced me to two small, elderly Irish gentlemen who were the managers. They were both very warm and friendly, immediately putting me at ease. They showed me a small room they had available, and I rented it on the spot.

My two Irish landlords took one look at me and decided I needed protectors. They assigned themselves to this task, and all the time I lived there, they hovered over me like a pair of old mother hens.

The day after moving into my new quarters, I walked down to the Blackfriar's Theater Guild on 59th Street. I had seen their newspaper ad and decided to check them out. The Guild was owned by a Catholic Diocese and run by Father Nagel and Father Carey, two Dominican priests. They put on Off Broadway productions and, once a year, a Lenten play.

Walking into their building, I took the elevator to the second floor as the ad directed. The strangest sensation came over me as the elevator doors opened and I stepped out. I had never been there before, yet it felt very familiar to me—as if I were coming home. Instinctively, I knew which way to walk down the hall and what door to open. Even before I was interviewed by Father Nagel and Father Carey, I knew I would be working for them. The two Fathers apparently had the same "feeling." No contract was drawn between us, nothing said, nothing signed; it was just somehow understood.

Now that I had a place to live and a place to work, I was ready to keep my second promise to myself. Leaving Blackfriar's Guild, I walked several blocks over to Fifth Avenue, feeling quite pleased with myself. Now I belonged! I was part of this city, and I had managed all on my own. *Not bad for a small-town gal!* I thought.

I sauntered along Fifth Avenue, window shopping and browsing in some of the stores. As I passed one shop window, a little black velvet hat on display caught my eye. It was a jaunty, tri-corner style with a long net sash that could either be tied under the chin or wrapped around to the back to form a bouffant bow and veil. I tried it on and fell in love with it. Handing it to the sales clerk to be boxed, I clenched my teeth and looked at the price tag. *Twenty-five dollars!* It was a good thing I had a job now.

I had only been in New York two days and already had kept two of my three promises: to kiss Times Square and to buy a hat on Fifth Avenue. Only one, the carriage ride on my opening night on Broadway, was left to go.

Jean in scene from "Mary of Magdala"
A Blackfriar's play

Chapter Six
Broadway—At Last!

The war had ended while I was in Boston, and soon after my arrival in New York City our servicemen came home. The city was filled with wild celebrations and ticker-tape parades. Hordes of people streamed down to Times Square to be part of the jubilant bedlam. Friends urged me to come along, but my emotions were very tangled. I was so very grateful the war was over—*Thank God it was*—but at such a devastating cost: lives lost, families and marriages torn apart. I thought of all the men I had met at the USO shows and hospitals where I had performed. There was so much pain in their eyes. Young kids, butchered, chewed up forever. And what about Roy? Had he made it home?

I felt guilty for not wanting to celebrate when the whole city was rejoicing, but I just couldn't. I turned and walked against the crowd, away from Times Square, where I could find a quiet place to remember the ones with shattered lives and bodies and those who had not returned.

The Blackfriar's Guild employed an office manager and a director. The performers were mostly volunteer, but from time to time, when I passed one of the Fathers in the hallway, he'd slip me some money. It usually averaged out to more than fair wages, which made me work hard to please them.

Here, my varied training in high school, little theater, and Summer and Winter Stock was really put to use. Not only did I act in their productions, I also helped design and decorate stage sets.

One such play was the Lenten production of "Mary of Magdala," in which I was cast as both a Grecian Lady and the dancing tumbler, Aletta. I enjoyed being involved in all aspects of a production, so when problems with the rental of historical costumes arose, I volunteered my services there as well.

As a result, I spent several days at the library researching the era of the play in order to design an authentic wardrobe. Then, for two weeks prior to opening night I never left the theater. When I wasn't sewing on the fifty-two different costumes required for the play, I was painting on the five elaborate frescoes I had helped create for the set. It was an exhausting but exhilarating time, that pushed my capabilities to the very limit. My efforts were well rewarded, however, when the play reviews came out.

Waiting to see what the critics have to say about a performance can be as nerve-wracking as opening night. After our first performance of "Mary of Magdala," the cast members gathered backstage and in the Theater Guild office, each of us bringing a copy of the New York Times, the Wall Street Journal, the Post, and any other newspapers that ran the reviews.

One review read, *"A Blackfriar newcomer, Miss Jean Lovelace, indicates marked versatility by her acting ability, her accurate and beautiful costumes, as well as her work on the sets."*

Another read, *"The set, worthy of any stage, has frescoes painted by the same Jean Lovelace who designed and executed the excellent costumes."*

I read the reviews over and over again, basking in their words of approval. It wasn't the first time I had been written up in a play review, but it was my first time to be written up for a New York City production. My dream of Broadway was coming closer and closer to reality.

In the early spring of 1947, the Chapel Playhouse, a Summer Stock company in Guilford, Connecticut, hired Dennis Gurney to direct their upcoming season. Directors often brought in their own full-season actors, while the leading parts were given to celebrities booked through their New York agents. Gurney had been the director at Blackfriar's Theater Guild while I was there. He showed the Guilford people my reviews and convinced them I should be their ingenue for the summer season. When he told me they had agreed, I could hardly catch my breath. I gulped and sputtered my acceptance as thankful tears filled my eyes. Here, at last, was my ticket into the Actor's

Union. This was another great moment in my life. Whatever was guiding my steps was again preparing the way, opening and closing doors for me along the way. I felt the same now as I had when I came to Blackfriar's Guild for the first time...as if it were all arranged and settled before I even arrived.

The ink was still wet on my contract when I took it down to the office of the Actor's Equity Association.

"How much is the membership fee?" I asked the clerk behind the counter as I held out my contract.

She told me the amount, and I opened my purse to count out the bills. Then I dumped my coins out on the counter. To my dismay, I was short one thin dime. I counted the money again. I looked at the woman in sheer agony.

"Here, Kid," she said. "I've got a dime!"

"Oh, thank you!" I gushed. "I'll pay you back." The clerk waved away my assurances, but I insisted. "I <u>will</u> pay you back—I have to!" I was so proud to finally be a member that I didn't want anyone else to have any part in it.

True to my word, when I returned to New York at the end of the summer, the first thing I did was head down to the Union office to pay back that clerk. She didn't even remember loaning me the dime. What had been a momentous occasion for me had been just another day at the office for her.

During that summer in Guilford, I had the opportunity to work with many Broadway actors and film stars, such as Roger Pryor, Diana Barrymore, Herschel Bentley, Freddie Bartholomew, and Jean Parker. Working with these well-known celebrities added status to my own acting resume.

It was also in Guilford that my ambition led me into a trap that would ensnare me for many years to come. There was a part I desperately wanted to play in "This Thing Called Love," a sophisticated comedy. However, the character I wanted to portray smoked, and I didn't. I knew it was next to impossible to fake smoking, so I asked some of the stage hands to give me a crash course in the "art." I wanted to have all the gestures and stances down pat before I tried out.

We went back stage and sat down on a pile of ropes, where my instruction began. After several cigarettes, the stage hands agreed I was smoking like an old pro.

"Fine!" I exclaimed. I stood up to leave and fell flat on my face, as dizziness and nausea enveloped me.

The part did become mine, but at a very high cost. After two weeks of smoking in rehearsals and the play, I was hooked. Thirteen years later I was desperate to quit, but by then I was smoking close to three packs a day. That afternoon when I commissioned the stage hands to teach me how to smoke, I had no idea of the intense battle I was setting myself up for later on in my life.

When Summer Stock closed, I returned to New York, full of anticipation. While making the rounds that fall, I ran into Ditter, a girl I had met at Priscilla Beach Playhouse. We were both looking for a place to live and agreed to share an apartment to cut down on expenses.

Ditter and I had learned the hard way that theater could be a very cutthroat business. Gathering at restaurants and cocktail parties, showmen and actors pressed each other for information regarding upcoming productions and auditions. Then everyone did their best to beat you to the auditions. By mutual consent, Ditter and I never talked about what parts we were interested in or trying out for; each morning we went our separate ways.

Two or three times a week, we would meet at the Cordial Rendezvous, a bar next to Radio City Music Hall. This was an important hangout for many people in show business. During the casual "Happy Hour," important contacts were made with significant agents, playwrights, actors, and an occasional director. It was also a meeting place for bookies and other "interesting" characters from various walks of life.

Without a doubt, I was rubbing shoulders with a fast crowd. Outwardly, I blended well and seemed to be just like them. I made the same rounds of cocktail parties and bars, listened and watched for the same opportunities, and nurtured the same dreams of success. But inwardly, we had little else in common. I was reluctant to pay the same price to achieve success that many of the others were paying all the time.

One late afternoon, I arrived at The Cordial before Ditter, and while I waited for her to show up, the waiter brought me a Brandy Alexander. This thick, rich drink, made with creme de cacao, ice cream and brandy, was a specialty I really enjoyed, but seldom ordered because my finances were so limited. Smiling, I asked the waiter who had sent it to me, and he pointed toward a man standing at the end of the bar. I had seen this fellow several times before. He nodded to me when I looked his way, and I raised my glass, smiling my thanks.

The next time I went into the bar, he sent another Alexander over to my table. This time, as he was leaving, he paused beside me and introduced himself as Jesse Goldstein. I smiled and asked how he knew I liked Alexanders.

He grinned. "I've seen you order them a time or two."

After that there was often a Brandy Alexander waiting to greet me when I arrived at the Cordial Rendezvous. I knew Jesse and his friend, Michael Weinberg, were bookies, besides holding down their regular jobs. Mike was a liquor union representative and Jesse was a night distribution chief for the <u>New York Times</u>. As we got better acquainted, I learned that these two had grown up together in the slums, often forced to eat from garbage cans. Now they were both married and doing quite well. I valued their friendship all the more because they never once made an improper advance toward me. Our rare friendship was open, honest, and loyal, and we were careful to keep it that way.

Once Jesse asked me if I was ever going to get married. I considered his question for a few minutes. "Well," I said, "if I ever do, it will have to be to someone I knew as a kid."

"Why?" he asked, puzzled.

"I want to marry someone I can have faith in—believe in. The men I've met here are too smooth. There's always an angle. I don't trust them..." My voice drifted off as I considered my words. For a moment Roy Zeiler flashed through my mind. It had been years since I had seen him. Funny I should think of him just now.

Jesse reached across the table and patted my hand. "Whoever he is, he'll be a lucky man."

Both men kept a watchful eye over me. "If you ever need anything, Jean, just let me or Mike know," Jesse told me one afternoon. I liked that. I felt safe when either of them was around, and one afternoon that feeling proved to be very valid.

I was waiting for Ditter to arrive when three men moved in on me. They were flashily dressed and obnoxious as they insisted I have a drink with them. I quietly declined their offer, but they slid into the booth with full assurance and brazenly told the waiter to bring me another "whatever-she-had-before." I insisted I didn't wish to drink any more. One of the trio patted my wrist with a hand flashing two large diamonds and a wrist watch worth more than everything I owned.

I didn't know quite what to do. They were overbearing and arrogant as they leered at me.

"Please, gentlemen," I began...

Just then the waiter appeared. "Excuse me, Miss Lovelace, but you are wanted on the phone. You can take the call in that booth."

Puzzled, but grateful for an excuse to get away from my captors, I followed him to the phone booth. As the waiter moved away I picked up the dangling receiver.

"I thought you might want an excuse to get away from your admirers," said a deep voice I immediately recognized as Jesse's. "Tell them you have to meet someone," he chuckled.

I thanked him profusely and hung up. *Bless him!* He was always there behind the scenes, watching out for me like a guardian angel.

My next acting job was with at the Sail Loft Theater, a Summer Stock company in Germantown, New York. During the first week of rehearsals, I discovered that our wages would be held up for two weeks. Realizing I would not have enough money to see me through to my first paycheck, I dialed the special number Jesse had given me to use in an emergency. When he answered, I asked if I could borrow some money until payday. He immediately wired me more than I asked for, along with a telegram that said, "FINAL PAYMENT ON RADIO. WE SURE LIKE IT. JESSE." Once again he was protecting my reputation from any possible gossips who might question why some man had wired me money. As soon as payday arrived, I gratefully sent back the loan.

When Summer Stock ended, I returned to New York and once again began making the rounds of the cocktail parties and theater hangouts in search of acting opportunities. One such party was being held at the penthouse of a countess living in Manhattan. I'd heard that several important theater people were going to be there, so my roommate, Ditter, and I decided to go.

When we arrived at the luxurious apartment, we were ushered in by a petite French maid who had obviously been crying. As she led us into the elegant living room, I wondered what had upset her so badly.

The room was filled with a gala crowd of people, and I joined a small group who were discussing their upcoming holiday plans. The countess asked what my plans were, and I said I was going to fly to Oregon to visit my folks.

"Oh, Dahling!" remonstrated the countess. "Don't say 'folks!' It's so-o-o colloquial!"

A humiliated flush crept into my cheeks. "If Steven Foster could write a song about 'old folks at home,'" I countered, "then it's good enough for me!"

"Well!" she breathed archly. "Really, now..."

A tense silence slowly settled over the group, but I was just warming up.

"You're so proper!" I said. "You don't even notice anyone you consider to be beneath you. I'll bet you don't have any idea why your little maid was crying tonight!"

"Crying?" she asked, clutching the pearls at her throat.

"Yes, she was very upset; but you didn't even notice, did you?" Everyone stood frozen like statues as I continued. "I'll bet you've never so much as spoken to your garbageman!"

Grabbing my coat, I quickly left the place before things got really out of hand—as if they hadn't already.

Several days later I was walking down the street when I heard someone call my name.

"Jean! Jean, Dahling—please!"

I turned around to see a limousine pulling up to the curb, the countess waving to me from the window. She began to climb from the car before it even stopped, knocking hat boxes out as she came. Her chauffeur rushed around to help her, but she waved him away. "Dahling! Please wait," she cried as she rushed up to me. "I must ask you to forgive me. You were right. I was rude, and it was dreadful of me. Oh! And I found out why my maid was crying!" Her words tumbled out breathlessly. "She'd had a tiff with her boyfriend. Everything's fine now. Really! And Jean! I spoke to my char man. He is a perfectly delightful person..." She gulped in a huge breath of air as she grasped my hand. "Please forgive me, Jean. Please!"

We parted friends that afternoon, and though I never saw the countess again, I always smile when she comes to mind.

One afternoon at the Cordial Rendezvous I heard that the motion picture actress Jean Parker was playing the lead in "Burlesque" opposite Bert Lahr at the Belasco Theater.

Parker and I had worked together in Guilford, Connecticut, and really liked each other. I went down to the Belasco hoping to see her and happened to catch her with a few free moments. As we chatted, she told me that "Burlesque" was due to go on a road tour in about seven weeks. She would be leaving the show then, due to other commitments, and Gail McKenzie would be playing the lead on the road.

"They need an understudy for the lead who can also dance and fill out the chorus line," Parker told me. "You should try out for it, since you know how to tap."

Jack Carlson, the Road Company Manager, just happened to be in the theater that afternoon, and Jean introduced us. He looked me up and down pretty thoroughly while she told him about my various abilities. Mr. Carlson said he would notify me when the auditions were to be held.

Back in my apartment, I reviewed the events of my whirlwind visit to the Belasco Theater. Would Mr. Carlson call, as he had said? Would this become my chance to be in a Broadway production? I tried not to get my hopes up too high, but excitement pulsed through every vein.

Two days later I received a message to contact Jack Carlson's office about an audition. It was to be held at a hotel, as I had heard they often were, and I dressed for it with great care, wishing to look exactly right. Show business had taught me that "looking the part" was half the battle. I really wanted this job and was very thankful for any edge my dancing might give me.

The hotel was an impressive one on Central Park South. I took the elevator up to the eighth floor and walked down the plushly carpeted hall to the room number I had been given. When I knocked on the door, a well-dressed man ushered me in. Carlson was standing by a large open sliding window overlooking the park. He smiled and introduced me to Bud Norton, the script and properties man. They mixed me a drink and told me to help myself to hors d'oeuvres.

"Am I the first to arrive?" I asked as I went over to the table. I was surprised by the small amount of food laid out. *Must be very few auditioning,* I thought, pleased that not too many would be trying out. It made the odds better for landing the part. I crossed my fingers hopefully.

The three of us made small talk for a few minutes, then Norton said he had to leave. Carlson had just mixed another drink, so he handed it to me and walked Norton to the door. They spoke in undertones for a moment, and then Carlson let him out. As he closed the door, he turned the lock. A flicker of uneasiness flashed through me. *Something was wrong.*

"Where are the others?" I asked again, my voice slightly higher than before.

"Never mind them," he said quietly. "They'll be along."

I suddenly realized how naïve I had been. "There aren't any others coming, are there?"

He smiled knowingly. "I'm giving you the part, Jean. Isn't that what you want?" He slowly looked me up and down.

"Without even trying out?" A seed of revulsion was taking root in the pit of my stomach.

"Jean Parker speaks very highly of you. That's good enough for me." His voice was a husky whisper now. "Come on, Kid..." He began to unbuckle his belt, no longer being coy.

My face flushed as I rose from my seat and backed away from him. The large, open window was behind me and, setting my drink on a coffee table, I slowly moved toward it. The revulsion was now in full bloom. *What made him think it would be this easy?*

"Come on, Jeannie," he cajoled, as he walked toward me. "You know what this is all about."

All at once nothing seemed to matter any more. My efforts, my hopes, dreams of Broadway, all my training...for this? Everything suddenly seemed ugly and dirty. It wasn't even that I was so virtuous; I just didn't want any part of this whole rotten mess. Without even thinking about it, I placed one foot on the ledge outside the sliding window.

"I came here to audition for the part," I said quietly. "Nothing more!" I felt ashamed for being so gullible.

"Come on, Kid..." His eyes were smoldering. "Get back in here."

"No, Mr. Carlson. "I'm leaving—either through the door or through this window." I distinctly spoke each word with my eyes glued to his face. "It's your choice." I felt ice cold.

He saw I meant it. Standing very still, he slowly shook his head. "Okay, Jean. Okay. Come back inside. I'm not going to do anything...I'm sorry, Kid." He backed away.

I kept my foot over the windowsill. "Unlock the door and get clear away from it." I felt sick and empty and dirty. All I wanted now was to get out.

He slowly backed away and unlocked the door. Then he sidled across to the opposite side of the room like a whipped puppy, looking ashamed as he fumbled to rebutton his pants. He tried to muster up a thread of composure by saying, "Come on, Jean. Forget it."

Watching him carefully, I stepped back inside the room, picked up my purse and hurried out the door. Once in the hallway I ran to the elevator and rang the call button. I felt like such a fool. I was desperate to put distance between Carlson and me and the whole stinking mess.

My opportunity to perform on Broadway had become an ugly, dirty nightmare. I was sure I would never see or hear from Jack Carlson again...but I was wrong.

He called the very next day, although I refused to talk to him. When he phoned a second time, my roommate convinced me to hear what he had to say. Grimacing, I took the receiver.

"Yes?" I asked shortly.

"If you want the part, Jean, come down to the Belasco Theater and sign the contract."

I didn't respond.

"You don't have to see me. I'll leave the contract at the box office. All you have to do is sign it, but I can't hold the part past 5:00 p.m."

I hung up the phone, unsure what to do. I sorely wanted the part, but didn't want to spend the season fighting off Carlson's unwelcome advances. I couldn't help wondering if this was just another trick.

Finally, just before five, I went down to the Belasco Theater. At the box office I asked the male attendant if there was a contract for me, and held my breath while he shuffled through a file folder. I still wondered if I was being duped.

"Here it is!" the man smiled, lifting out a sheet of paper. "Sign it at the table in the lobby."

He pressed a button to release the locked doors, and I took the contract inside to where two men were seated at a long, narrow table near an aisle entrance. They were evidently expecting me, because one asked, "Are you Jean Lovelace?"

"Yes, Sir."

He handed me a pen and some documents. While they both watched, I signed my first contract to perform in a Broadway production. Then they also signed and told me to report for rehearsal the next morning at 9:00. As I left the lobby I glanced around, halfway expecting Carlson to appear, but he kept his word and stayed out of sight.

Sometimes I felt like pinching myself to see if I was awake or sleeping. To actually have reached my greatest dream—acting on Broadway—seemed too incredible to be true. *Jean Lovelace, Broadway Actress*, I'd whisper to myself and then laugh out loud.

Every minute of rehearsal was pure bliss. I spent every spare moment at the theater, soaking up the aura that surrounds a Broadway production in the works. When the two leads, Jean Parker and Burt Lahr, danced, I stood back of the scenery, watching their silhouettes twirl on the backdrop. I memorized their routines, pretending it was me with Bert, copying every gesture and step.

"Burlesque" was a long running show—it had been playing for almost three years in New York when I signed my contract—but for me the true opening night was the night of my first performance.

When the curtain came down on my opening night, it was time to keep my third and final promise to myself—the carriage ride. Some of my friends wanted to accompany me, but I refused. This night was for me, alone. Arranging to meet them later at the apartment, I left the theater and walked toward Central Park and the carriages waiting there. I wore a formal and a borrowed evening cape, and as I walked up the street I was too excited to feel the cold even though it was snowing lightly.

At the park entrance, I found just the hansom cab I wanted, round like Cinderella's carriage, and pulled by a magnificent white horse. Walking up to the warmly-dressed driver, I smiled. "Is your carriage available for once around the park?"

"Yes, indeed!" the kindly old man said as he climbed down from his seat. He helped me up the steps into the carriage, and as I sat down, I loosened my cape so I could spread my full-skirted gown wide across the seat. I leaned back into the tufted leather upholstery. Its rich smell mingled with the crisp night air, and I inhaled deeply as the driver mounted his seat and flicked the reins.

Frost made the trees appear to have been dusted with silver, and stars glittered in the black sky overhead as we clip-clopped elegantly over the little bridges and through the park. I gazed at the warm glow of city lights that twinkled through the trees. New York didn't know it, but tonight it belonged to me.

When my ride ended, the driver let down the steps of the carriage and started to assist me down. I smiled, and suddenly felt compelled to confide in him.

"You don't know it, Sir, but I've traveled 3,000 miles and waited three years for this ride."

"Where are you from, child?" he asked.

"Portland, Oregon!" I laughed and told him about my three promises: to kiss Times Square, to buy a hat on Fifth Avenue and to take this ride in a hansom cab on my opening night. "Tonight's the night, Sir!"

He shook his head in amazement. "Where do you live now?"

When I told him, he said, "Well, climb right back inside, child. I'm not letting you walk home tonight."

"Oh, no! I can't!" I protested. "I don't have enough money."

"This part's on me!" He bowed grandiosely, closed the carriage door, and climbed up on his seat. With another flick of the reins, we were off again. He took me right to my door, and with a final dramatic flourish, helped me down from the carriage. Beaming my thanks, I paid him his fee, then stood on the steps of my apartment, watching until he disappeared into the night. There are kind people everywhere.

Up in my room, several friends were waiting. There we celebrated my opening night in a manner more befitting my means: hot dogs and coffee.

"Burlesque" played on Broadway for two more weeks, before we took it on the road. During that time, a Merchant

Marine vessel docked in New York. A seaman named Roy Zeiler came ashore with some buddies and headed uptown looking for a show. When they came to the Belasco Theater, they stood outside reading the program that was on display.

"Hey!" Roy suddenly yelped. "Jean Lovelace! I know her!"

"Aw, sure you do!" laughed his buddies.

"No, really!" he said, scarcely believing it himself. He shook his head. "She always said she'd make it to Broadway someday. Looks like she did."

They decided to buy tickets for the show. Afterwards, Roy's friends tried to talk him into going backstage, but he refused. It had been eight years since he had seen me.

"Naw. She wouldn't be interested in seeing me now." He returned to his ship without even calling me. Soon, thousands of miles were again between us; but unbeknownst to us both, our worlds were soon to collide in a most unexpected way.

Touring with a Broadway Production was an exhausting cycle of packing, unpacking, rehearsing, and performing as we played in fifteen cities across the country. One of our scheduled appearances was at the Ford Theater in Baltimore, Maryland.

I was leaving the theater late one night after the performance when I noticed Bert Lahr, the male lead in "Burlesque," standing alone under the theater marquee.

"Hey, Lovelace! Come here."

I walked over to him, and he pointed down the street. "Look down there as far as you can and tell me what you see."

I wasn't sure what he was getting at. It was dark, and I couldn't see much of anything. "Well, the burlesque houses are down there on Skid Row..." I hesitated.

"Yep! That's it, Lovelace. It's twenty-seven blocks from those houses down there to the Ford Theater here. That's where I started, Lovelace. It took me twenty-seven years to make it, but here I am, playing in the top theater in Baltimore. Twenty-seven years to come twenty-seven blocks." He was enjoying this moment of reminiscence.

We stood in silence staring down the long dark street until he nudged my shoulder. "See you tomorrow, Lovelace," he said, and disappeared into the night.

Gail McKenzie had taken over the female lead just before "Burlesque" went on the road. Although Jean Parker and I had worked together as friends, I didn't have a warm relationship with Gail. She maintained a cool distance between us, in spite of my repeated efforts to be friendly.

One afternoon I was rehearsing Gail's dance routines on stage when she and Bert Lahr walked through the theater. Bert stopped to watch me dance for a few minutes, then left Gail standing in the aisle while he came down to the stage.

"Where'd you learn those steps?" he asked.

"From back there, watching your silhouettes when you dance," I explained. Bert grinned.

"No kidding!" He jumped up on the stage. "Do it again with me from the top," he said, holding out his hand.

I took his hand, and together we danced through the entire routine, our bodies in perfect sync. It was as if we had been dancing together forever. When the music ended, we were both breathless. "You're good, Kid!" he laughed. "Really good! That was a lot of fun."

My feet were still now, but my heart continued to dance as Bert walked back up the aisle to rejoin Gail. The glare that she flashed over her shoulder as they left the theater did nothing to dampen the enthusiasm I felt.

I paid a steep price for that brief dance with Bert. From that moment on Gail saw me as an enemy, a threat to her in some way. She was determined never to let me play her part, not even one night when she was so ill with a cold and laryngitis she could scarcely speak.

"Burlesque" was scheduled to play in Portland, Oregon, and I had been looking especially forward to that. It is customary to let understudies perform the lead in a matinee performance when the show plays in their home town. Now, however, I was almost certain Gail would never let me play the part—not even in Portland. It was clear I had come to a dead end with this road company.

I had been offered a contract playing the leads for The Shady Lane Playhouse in Marengo, an Illinois Summer Stock company, but I didn't know what I should do. Canceling a contract in the middle of a road company tour was an unpardonable sin in show business. No one would hire you after that. Finally I went to Bert Lahr for advice.

"Do you think there is any chance at all that Gail will let me play the lead while we're on the road—even in Portland?"

He shook his head. "Jean, Gail's never going to let you do that part."

I explained then about the offer I had received.

"If you have a chance to play leads somewhere, Jeannie, I'd take it," he said. "And I'll see to it that you suffer no repercussions from quitting our show on the road. We're almost through with the tour, anyway."

I appreciated his kindness.

Following Bert's suggestion, I resigned from the road company when we finished our run in Chicago and left for Merengo, Illinois, where my new contract was with the Shady Lane Playhouse.

Usually, actors and actresses stayed in private homes while they were playing Summer Stock. In Marengo, I stayed in the home of a very prominent couple who were active in promoting the arts in their city.

For me, the best time to memorize my part was in the wee, small hours of the morning while the rest of the world slept. About 3:30 one morning I was propped up in bed with a thermos of black coffee beside me, memorizing my lines, when my host walked into my room.

"I heard you get up," he said softly. "I thought I'd check on you." He came over and sat down on the edge of my bed.

"Where's your wife?" I asked mildly.

"She left today to go visit her sister. She won't be back for a couple of weeks." He paused and then patted my arm. "I get awfully lonesome sometimes..."

Sitting in bed with only my thin gown on made me feel like an animal caught in a trap. I didn't want to insult this gentleman, but on the other hand, I had no intentions of following his lead. Frantically I tossed around for a "polite" escape.

"You know," I said brightly, "I sure could use a good cup of fresh coffee."

He looked pointedly at the thermos beside me.

"Oh, that's cold!" I waved it away. "Doesn't fresh coffee sound good?"

While he went to make it, I jumped into some clothes and hurried to the kitchen. After that, I always made sure my bedroom door was locked.

I was frequently accused of being "holier-than-thou" because I didn't party and play around, as so many of the other cast members did. It wasn't that I was never tempted to give in to some of the invitations I received. It was just that I had seen what happened to the people who did. Invariably, their brief moment of pleasure turned into long-term misery. I was determined to avoid that for myself, but it meant some lonely times. Often I felt just as I had the summer after my parents divorced, when I didn't seem to belong anywhere.

A professional formal portrait

Chapter Seven
A Change in Plans

Back in New York, during the early spring of 1949, I decided to go home to Oregon for a visit. I had signed a new contract for the coming Summer Stock season, but rehearsals wouldn't begin until the last of May.

Jessie Goldstein volunteered to take me to the airport, and as we waited for my plane to depart, he suddenly asked, "Jeannie? Are you sure you'll be coming back to New York?"

I turned toward him in surprise. "Of course, Jesse. I've already signed a Summer Stock contract. Why did you ask me that?"

He didn't reply, just stared at me for several moments before looking away.

When it was time to board the plane, Jesse handed me a copy of *Harper's Bazaar* that he'd brought with him. "Here's something for you to read on the plane. There's a real good article on page forty-two." He hugged me then. "If I don't see you again, Kid, I really enjoyed it."

Not until the plane was in the air did I open the magazine to page forty-two. There I found two twenty-dollar bills. *He's still watching out for me*, I thought with a smile. Thumbing through the magazine, I mulled over his last remark to me. *Why had he asked me if I'd be coming back? Of course he'd be seeing me again.*

Mom and Ben were waiting for me at the airport when my plane arrived. As we drove to their home, I leaned back in my seat and took a deep breath, exhaling slowly. The life I had made for myself in New York was very different from the one I had known here; New York was exhilarating, but also demanding and intense. It was always good to come back to the slower pace of life in Oregon. The upcoming two weeks stretched pleasantly before me.

I stayed with Mom and Ben for a few days, then took the city bus over to see Dad and his new wife, Clara. I had only been in their home a short time when the telephone rang.

I reached for the phone and in my best impersonation of a maid in a Broadway production, said, "Good afternoon, Mr. Lovelace's residence." Dad smiled and raised his eyebrows.

"May I please speak to Mr. Lovelace?" asked a deep, resonant, male voice.

I covered the mouthpiece with my hand. "Dad! It's for you. *Real nice voice!*"

Dad answered and immediately handed the phone back. "It's for *you*, Honey."

Somewhat irritated, I took the phone, wondering who it could be. I always kept my visits home a secret because, some of my childhood acquaintances were overly impressed with my acting career, and that embarrassed me.

"You'll never guess who this is!" said that deep voice.

"All right," I said, straining to be polite, "who is it?"

"Roy...Roy Zeiler!"

My heart skipped a beat. "Roy! Where are you?" I was incredulous. "How did you find me?" This was unreal!

"I saw you on the bus a few minutes ago. Can I come see you?"

"Sure!" I laughed in amazement. "Any time."

"I'll be there in twenty minutes!"

I laid the phone down and raced towards the bedroom to change. Rummaging through my suitcase, I looked for something suitable to wear. The theater had taught me the art of "quick changing," and I put it to good use now, changing outfits four times before he arrived.

When the doorbell rang, I raced breathlessly to the front hall, stopping for one final pat. Opening the door, I noticed that a gentle snow had begun to fall, and the flakes were landing softly on Roy's broad shoulders. How tall he looked—how handsome in his fine suit and topcoat! The skinny boy with the protruding Adam's apple had disappeared, and in his place was this strong, powerful, good-looking man.

We reached out for each other's hands and stood there on the porch grinning in delight. In those very first moments it seemed as if all the shoddiness and dirt of our world fell away, and we were just kids again—as pure and innocent as the snow falling around us. I had a wild urge to kiss him—so sure it would be right, and yet so afraid it might be wrong. I did nothing, not wanting to spoil this beautiful moment.

"Well, doggone!" he finally chuckled softly.

"Well, doggone!" I agreed, still breathless.

"Well, doggone!" bellowed Dad from inside the house. "Come on in and close the door. It's cold out there!"

I didn't find out until much later that Roy had gone home that same afternoon and broken off his relationship with a young woman he had been dating for two years. "I don't know if Jean will have me," he told her, "but I want to be available if she will." That evening Roy came back, and the next five days passed in a breathtaking whirl.

Every afternoon, while Dad and Clara were at work, Roy came over to see me. We sat together in the kitchen sipping coffee, catching up on each other's lives. Roy had sailed around the world the equivalent of nine times since I had seen him. He told me about being in New York and seeing me on stage. I asked why he hadn't come backstage.

"I had a boat to catch," he teased. From New York he told me he had sailed down the East Coast, making several ports along the way, then through the Panama Canal and up the West Coast to Seattle. After disembarking, he headed for Portland for a quick visit. On the morning I took the bus to Dad's house, Roy's rented car had had a flat tire. He coasted into a parking spot and got out just as a city bus stopped. He jumped aboard, thinking he would go home and call a repairman. It just happened to be the same bus I was on.

I shook my head in amazement as I listened to him. From opposite ends of the continent, from one coincidence after another, Roy and I had both ended up in Portland *on the same city bus* at the very same time. That one incident, more than any other in my life, convinced me there is no such thing as a "coincidence."

Such different lives we had lived, such varied pathways we had followed; yet now, sitting across from each other at that tiny kitchen table, it was as if we had never been apart.

Each night I dressed up in my Broadway finery, and we would go out on the town. Roy was an excellent dancer, and on more than one occasion the dance floor cleared while we pivoted around and around in the center of a circle of admiring people. We knew we were a dashing twosome and loved every minute of it.

One night over a candlelit dinner in a romantic little Italian restaurant, I looked Roy in the eyes. "I don't suppose you'd ever quit the sea...?"

He met my gaze, unblinking. "Try me."

We both laughed awkwardly and quickly changed the subject, hesitant to take it any further. We were spending every spare moment together, but Roy had yet to kiss me or tell me if he was feeling the same way I was.

On the fourth day, Roy again came over to Dad's house in the afternoon. The next day would be our last one together. Then I would fly back to New York, and Roy's ship would leave for an eighty-seven-day South American voyage.

As we sat at the little kitchen table, the phone rang for Roy. When he turned around after hanging up the receiver, I was standing beside the table, blocking his path. "I have to be at the dock to sign papers at six," he explained.

I didn't move, and neither of us spoke. We just stared at each other while my heart pounded.

"Jean," Roy murmured, "I don't know what to say."

I shrugged slowly, never taking my eyes off him. "Why say anything?"

Suddenly, he pulled me close and wrapped me in his arms. And finally, after four interminable days of waiting, we kissed each other. No romance novel has ever come close to describing the thrill of that moment. This was what I had been waiting for. This was why I had shunned casual romance so many times, in so many places. Without even knowing it, I had been waiting for Roy.

He held me away for a moment. "I don't suppose you'd ever quit the stage."

I grinned. "Try *me!*"

We were both trembling now, so full of emotion. "Jean, will you marry me?"

I nodded, almost afraid to speak. Swallowing, I said, "Roy, this is really going to change our lives..."

"Yeah," he said, "and I want it to."

We made a pact then, that I would quit the stage and Roy would quit the sea. We agreed that a marriage hadn't much chance on opposite sides of the world.

The next day, while Roy stood beside me, I phoned New York and canceled my acting contract. Then I called Ditter and asked her to ship my things home. My hand trembled as I hung up the phone. Broadway had been a lifelong dream. I had worked very hard to make it a reality. Canceling contracts meant I could never go back, but I knew it had to be all or nothing. I loved the stage too much to keep the door open, even a little bit. I was determined to give our marriage everything I had. I didn't want anything to interfere, and that meant I had to turn my back on the theater. If it didn't work, at least I would know I had given it everything I had. It had to be all or nothing.

Roy was committed to this one last trip with the Merchant Marines. I went down to the docks the next morning to see him off. As the ship's horn bellowed and the huge vessel moved away, panic seized me.

Oh Jean! I thought. *What have you done? What if he changes his mind? Have you been a complete fool?* It suddenly crossed my mind that Roy hadn't given up anything yet.

I shook my head to dispel the negative thoughts. There was much to do while he was gone. First, I had to find a job. I might as well get started.

Leaving the docks, I went straight to Tom Taylor's mechanical engineering firm in downtown Portland.

"Got a desk for me?" I asked as I walked in.

We hadn't seen each other since I had moved to California, but he showed no surprise at all. He just pointed toward a desk and drafting table in the corner. I walked over and sat down.

"Are you serious, Jean?" he asked then. "What about acting?"

"I'm getting married, Tom! I'm through acting."

"Then the job is yours. Welcome back."

Next, I needed a place to live. I found a small third-floor walk-up apartment, and since the landlord would only rent to married people, I rented it under the name of Mr. and Mrs. Roy Zeiler.

Roy was gone for eighty-seven days, and I wrote him eighty-seven letters. In return I received seven one-page epistles that basically said, *"How are you? I am fine. Write soon. Love, Roy."* The days dragged by as I swung between blissful happiness and abject misery and doubt. I couldn't wait for him to return.

Roy and Jean's Wedding Day

At last, on the evening of June nineteenth, Roy called from Seattle, Washington. His ship had docked, and he was flying to Portland. The plane would arrive at 5:00 the next morning.

As planned, I called Dad and Clara and, as soon as Roy got off the plane, the four of us headed for the Courthouse in Vancouver, Washington, where there was no waiting period for a marriage license. By 10:00 that morning Roy and I were pronounced husband and wife by the little Methodist minister who officiated. Dad and Clara threw rice on us to celebrate.

After a wedding breakfast for four, Roy and I drove to the apartment I had rented. Holding hands, we walked up the first two flights of stairs. On the second-floor landing, Roy swept me into his arms and carried me up the last flight. We started giggling at the trail of rice we were leaving behind us on the stairs as it trickled from my hair. Tenants peeked out of their doorways to see what the commotion was all about. We laughed all the more.

Inside our apartment Roy spun me around and around the room, then plopped me down on the bed. With a huge crash, it split into a pile of kindling. Things were off to a great start!

Roy got a job driving for Broadway Cab Company, and I continued drafting for Tom Taylor. On the side, we began buying small fixer-upper houses and lived in them as we re-modeled them. Being a draftsman, I also started drawing house plans, and we built three of these from the ground up. The engineers in Tom's office helped me iron out any heating, plumbing or architectural problems. Our bank account was growing nicely, and we were quite pleased with the way our life was going. Neither of us had any regrets about what we had given up. Together, we had so much more.

Jean at drafting table in a large office

June 1949
Roy and Jean walking down
Broadway in Portland

Chapter Eight
A Prayer, A Bible and A Ranch

Roy had a tremendous love for the outdoors. Many of our weekends were spent fishing or hunting. Although I thoroughly enjoyed our hunting trips, fishing was another matter. We would get up early Saturday morning and head for some little-known stream way up in the mountains. After what seemed to me like *miles* of hiking, Roy would find a spot that looked good and cast his fishing line. I would barely get myself settled into a comfortable spot nearby when he would reel in the line and say, "Come on, Honey! Let's go a little further upstream."

Roy was six feet tall compared to my modest five-feet four. He could jump logs and ford streams effortlessly, while I spent the entire time shinnying up one embankment and sliding down another in a constant game of "catch-up." My sense of humor waned sharply on these outings, as we went from fishing hole to fishing hole to fishing hole.

Finally, to our mutual relief, I began staying home and letting Roy fish alone or with a buddy more able to keep up with him. However, this meant I spent every weekend during fishing season by myself. To pass the time, I enrolled in a commercial art correspondence course.

It felt wonderful to be drawing again, putting my artistic skills to use. Each weekend I sat at our dining room table with my art supplies spread around me and worked on my assignments. I was getting excellent grades and learning art skills that I hadn't known I was capable of. Everything went quite well until fishing season ended. Since my art course was still going on, it was now Roy who was left to his own devices on the weekends.

One evening, as I sat immersed in my drawing, I glanced up to see Roy scowling over a pair of socks he was darning, exuding discontentment in every jab of the needle as he glared at me.

Okay, Jean, I thought to myself, *are you going to be an artist or a wife?* I knew my tendency to get caught up in whatever I was doing to the exclusion of everything else. If I were really going to give our marriage my very best effort, perhaps it was best to let my art class go. This would be the first thing I had ever set out to do that I had failed to finish. Even today, that thought sometimes bothers me.

The following week I wrote my instructors that I would not be completing the course, then wistfully put away my art portfolio and supplies. Even though I thought Roy was being a little selfish, I was determined to put our marriage first.

I was very grateful for my job with Tom Taylor's engineering firm. Besides the satisfying rapport I had with Tom and the other engineers in the office, it provided me an outlet for my creative bent. Portland was expanding rapidly, and our office was working with the larger architectural firms on many of the major buildings downtown, as well as the schools and hospitals that we specialized in.

Ivan Saunders, one of Tom's top engineers, had been with the firm nearly as long as I had. Although he was very quiet and unassuming, I had a deep respect for him. He was easy to work with, and always willing to lend his expertise where needed. The fact that he was a Christian fascinated me. He did not fit the Christian stereotype I had. He wasn't judgmental, preachy, or holier-than-thou. He was kind, with a quiet sense of humor, always dependable and gentle. Without fail, every day before he opened his sack lunch, he quietly bowed his head and prayed. This had earned him the nicknames "Deacon" or "Parson" around the office.

The day I jokingly referred to Ivan's book of specifications as his Bible did not strike me as being a pivotal day in my life. I was just trying to be funny, as I joked around with the other engineers. I didn't realize that when Ivan quietly said, "Jean, this is not my Bible," he was pointing me to a path that would change my life forever.

That night after Roy and I had finished dinner, I was cleaning up the dishes. I looked over to where he sat with his newspaper.

"Roy, would you mind if I bought a Bible?"

He looked up startled, and then roared with laughter. "You—buy a Bible?"

Somehow, his laughter felt like a slap in the face. I had not expected that reaction. "Roy, please, don't laugh!" For no reason at all, I burst into tears.

"Jean!" He leaped to his feet, realizing he had hurt me. "Honey, I didn't mean it...!" He wrapped his arms around me and lifted my chin. "Sure, you can buy a Bible." Then he added gruffly, "Just don't go overboard, okay? Don't get carried away...none of that fanatic stuff."

The very next day on my lunch hour I went to a large downtown bookstore to buy my first Bible. I thought there would be a small table with a few Bibles displayed, but the clerk directed me to an entire room that was full of them. I hadn't realized there were so many different kinds. Having no idea which was best, I finally settled on one with index tabs and good illustrations. And, just to be a little rebellious, I chose a bright red one. It didn't look quite so "religious." At $13.95, it was the most expensive book I had ever purchased up to that time.

Walking back to the office, I kept switching the bag from one hand to the other as if it were burning me. I felt as if the whole city knew what I was carrying in that bag. Once inside the office, I walked over to my desk and lit a cigarette to calm my nerves. Then I took the box holding the Bible out of the bag.

Taking it over to Ivan's drafting table I said, "Ivan, I bought a book..."

He looked up at me, puzzled.

"Please, Ivan," I said, pushing the box across his table, "open it."

Never taking his eyes off my face, he smiled as he reached out for the box and raised the lid. With all my smoking, he probably thought I was showing him a copy of *Tobacco Road*. Finally he looked down at the book, and I thought he was never going to look up again. When he did, his eyes were full of tears.

His open emotion embarrassed and rattled me. "I promise I'll read it from cover to cover," I stammered. "If God is in it, Ivan, I'll find Him, but I have to do it my own way."

He nodded. "May I make one suggestion, Jean?"

"Just one," I conceded.

"Would you mind starting with John?"

John? I thought. *Harry, Joe, Pete...why not?* Aloud I said, "Okay," and quickly walked back to my drafting table.

That night, after Roy had gone to bed, I sat in our kitchen with a pot of black coffee, a pack of cigarettes, and my new red Bible. "*Start with John,*" Ivan had said. Thumbing back and forth through the pages, I found three little Johns at the back of the book, but somehow I didn't think they were the ones he had meant. I was sure it had to be bigger than those. I kept looking and discovered a Saint Matthew, Mark, and Luke, followed by Saint John. Although Ivan had not said "saint," I assumed this was the John he had meant. It seemed like a strange place to start reading a book. You would lose the whole plot by starting three-quarters of the way through it. Still, taking a sip of coffee, I began to read.

"In the beginning was the Word, and the Word
was with God, and the Word was God. The same
was in the beginning with God. All things were
made by him and without him was not any thing
made that was made. In him was life and the life
was the light of men..."

The hours melted away as I read page after page, fascinated by the words. Much of it did not make sense, yet I somehow knew I was reading absolute truth. My coffee grew cold, and my cigarette turned to ash as I read on, unable to stop.

"*Jean!*" Roy's voice pierced my concentration. "Are you ever coming to bed?" I looked at the clock, shocked to see how long I had been reading. Reluctantly, I shut my Bible and went to bed.

After that, each evening after dinner while Roy read the newspaper, I read my Bible. I was finding it harder and harder to put it down. Roy started going to bed without me while I kept finishing one more chapter. I knew he was getting annoyed and didn't want him to accuse me of becoming a fanatic, so I began taking a small flashlight and my Bible to bed with me. As soon as Roy started breathing heavily, I pulled the covers over my head, turned on my flashlight and opened my Bible. My glasses steamed up, but I stealthily wiped them off and continued to read. If Roy moved, I would quickly douse the light.

One night, I was so engrossed that I got out of bed, went into the bathroom, and sat on the edge of the chilly tub as I shivered my way through page after page.

I found the bus ride to work to be a perfect time to read, although I discovered people were reluctant to share a seat with me as long as the Bible was open on my lap. They would stand in the aisle rather than sit down next to me. One morning, when the bus was particularly full, a young man in the back pushed his way toward the front where I sat. Plopping down in the empty seat beside me he said, "No point in our spoiling two seats." Smiling, he opened a Bible.

"Oh!" I laughed in delight. "Where are you reading?"

"I'm in Jeremiah. Where are you?"

We visited together, and I noticed the people around us had begun to eavesdrop on our conversation, smiling at our enthusiasm over our Bibles. The young man told me he was going to barber college.

"You'd be surprised how well you can witness when you have someone in the chair and a straight-edge razor in your hand."

Everyone around us laughed. Somehow we had gone from being pariahs to near celebrities on that bus. When I got off at my stop, I turned to wave to my new friend and saw the whole bus waving back. Even the gruff old driver was grinning.

Within a year I had read the Bible straight through three times, but still had no desire to go to church. I was suspicious of all denominations, not knowing which one was right. Ivan seemed to understand I was not ready for that step yet. He just quietly encouraged me in my Bible reading.

During hunting seasons, Roy and I would load our little pickup and head off to various remote parts of Oregon. Sometimes we went to the coast, other times to southern Oregon, but more and more often we went toward the eastern part of the state. Occasionally, Iris's new husband, Dave, went with us. He and Iris were living in Colorado now, but Dave loved eastern Oregon so much, he was considering buying a ranch there. In fact, he asked Roy to go with him to look at some places that were for sale. Dave did not find a ranch to his liking, but Roy came home rhapsodizing about one he had found in the John Day Country.

"It's so beautiful, Jean! So peaceful and remote—you would love it!"

I had my doubts. I liked the city. But I smiled and nodded my head to humor him. "Yes, Dear."

Roy talked of nothing else after that, describing to me the quaint little town of Dayville near where the ranch was located and his dream to become a rancher someday.

"But, Roy," I would reason, "we're city people! We know nothing about ranching."

"Honey, I *love* that place! And I want a ranch." His voice had a determined tone to it.

Roy and Dave paid another visit to the ranch, this time taking a whole roll of film to show me.

"Look at this, Jean!" he said excitedly, handing me one snapshot after another. "Have you ever seen such beautiful land?"

I looked at the dry, sagebrush-dotted land and thought that Yes, as a matter of fact, I *had* seen much, *much* more beautiful land. He pointed to a bedraggled, overgrown orchard surrounded by a tumble-down fence.

"Look! There's even a fruit orchard, Honey! We could raise our own fruit!"

My heart sank deeper with every picture he showed me. What I saw did not strike me as the Utopia Roy declared it to be. I could not imagine what had gotten into him.

"And here is the house!" he said with a flourish, as he handed me another snapshot.

"Roy!" I squeaked in dismay. *"That's the house?"* I was looking at a *shack*—an ancient, rickety, rundown, worm-eaten cabin!

"Yep!" Roy grinned happily. "See, you go outside and climb up this ladder here to get to the bedroom..."

I stared at him, flabbergasted, and Roy burst into laughter.

"Just kidding, Jean. That's the old, original homestead cabin." He handed me another picture. "Here's the real house."

I was so relieved, anything would have looked good to me then, which is exactly what he had planned.

"Okay, Honey," I finally sighed, sensing this was one battle I was destined to lose. "Just how big is this place?"

"It's just shy of 3,000 acres," he beamed.

I nearly dropped through the floor. It sounded as if he was wanting to buy all of eastern Oregon! After that, I decided it was time to go over there with Roy and see this "Shangri-La" for myself.

In 1954 the population of Dayville reached the sum total of 254 people. A stone schoolhouse sat atop a small hill in the middle of town. Stretched out below were two cafes, two gas stations, two churches and two stores. That was about all there was to Dayville. Looking out the car window as we drove through town, I nearly laughed aloud. *This was where Roy wanted to live?*

The ranch he had fallen in love with lay three miles east of Dayville and a mile off the highway. Climbing from the car, Roy grabbed my hand and started showing me around. We inspected the house, the old homestead cabin, and other outbuildings. We strolled through the overgrown orchard and walked out across the fields. Down by the John Day River, I slipped off my shoes and dabbled my feet in the chilly current while Roy kept up a steady commentary about all the things we could do here. As much as I did not understand what was pulling him in this direction, his enthusiasm was catching. By the time we headed back to Portland, I agreed that maybe we should make an offer on the place.

After several months of dickering back and forth with Lucille George, the ranch owner, a deal was struck. Roy and I went to visit our banker and tell him what we were doing. He stared at us in shocked disbelief.

"No! You two can't want to buy a ranch," he insisted. "Why, you're city folk!" He looked at Roy. "You're just starting to make a name for yourself around here with your building, Roy. Ranchers go broke!"

Roy and one of his horses

I cringed at his words, hearing the truth in them, but I knew they had sailed right over Roy's head. Undaunted, Roy told the banker we were selling our present house for the down payment. When we walked out of the bank, the deal was settled. We were on our way to becoming ranchers. I could have sworn there was now a subtle "cowboy" swagger to Roy's gait.

We decided to stay in Portland for three more years, while leasing the ranch out to a family in the Dayville area. During that time we would save every penny we could to pay off the ranch as much as possible. We also needed enough money to buy some livestock and a grubstake.

Roy fussed and fumed his way through two long years. We continued to build and redecorate older houses as much as time allowed from our regular jobs. We sold a couple of lots that we had acquired and even built one small cottage for a retired couple. Finally, after figuring and refiguring, I told Roy I thought we were far enough along to make it on one salary. "I can continue to work in Portland another year," I suggested, "and you can go ahead and move up to the ranch and get things started there…"

Roy began packing before the words were even out of my mouth.

On Christmas Eve of 1956, when Roy was thirty-seven and I was thirty-six, we loaded our old truck with all our belongings and headed east across the Cascade Mountains to Dayville, Oregon. On top of the truck was a huge Christmas tree I had insisted we bring along. Lady, our black Labrador retriever, was as excited as Roy when we set forth on this great new adventure. My excitement was tempered as I prayed we were not moving too soon.

Winter was much colder on the east side of the mountains. When we arrived at the ranch, we hastily built fires in the wood cook stove and the massive old living-room fireplace. Then, still bundled up in heavy coats and gloves, we decorated our Christmas tree to the music of the crackling flames and our cheap little radio.

The tree was decorated, and Roy and I had just sat down to exchange our gifts, when someone knocked on the door. It was Don and Jim Moore from the adjoining ranch, inviting us down to share Christmas Eve with their families. We were amazed at the kindness of these people to total strangers. We gave Lady her Christmas bone to chew on while we were gone and accompanied the Moore brothers down the road to their ranch.

As we walked through the door, we were immediately plunged into the festivities of an old-fashioned Christmas. A huge oak table sagged beneath platters of popcorn balls, homemade candies, nuts, cakes, oranges, and every other treat imaginable. Squealing children of all sizes ran in and out among laughing adults. Beribboned packages spilled out from under a lopsided Christmas tree.

"Mother Moore," as she was called by most everyone in Dayville, wiped her hands on her apron as she came from the kitchen to welcome us. Later, we would learn that she had been left a widow with seven young children to raise during the Depression. The children were grown now with families of their own, but they were all here tonight, squeezed beneath the roof of their old home place. Throughout the evening, other neighbors dropped in, and by the time the festivities wound down in the wee, small hours of the morning, Roy and I felt as if we'd met all of Dayville. We probably had...and we weren't "strangers" anymore.

We spent the rest of the holidays unpacking and getting settled in. Soon it was time for me to go back to Portland. Sunday night about 10:30, we drove into Dayville to wait for the bus.

"I sure hate for you to leave," Roy sighed. "It's going to be lonesome here without you."

I hugged his arm. "I know, Honey, but my working is the only way we can do this, and it's only for a year or so. We can hang in there that long." We hugged, trying to reassure each other that this was the best plan to follow.

Jean and Roy leaning on fence at Pioneer Grave

The bus arrived, and Roy gave me a quick kiss. "I'll see you next Friday morning," he said.

Climbing on the bus, I settled into a seat near the front. It felt strange to be leaving Roy behind in Dayville. I had made arrangements with Tom Taylor to work four ten-hour days a week. That way I could catch the midnight bus to Dayville on Thursday and have three days to spend at the ranch. It would be a rugged schedule, but it was the only way to make Roy's dream come true.

The ranch hadn't yet become my dream the way it was Roy's, but it was starting to. The time I had spent there so far had been wonderful. The easygoing simplicity of the people we had met had been like a tonic. There people meant what they said—even little things—small words you could build a mountain on. I had found our neighbors to be solid, real, and kind. As I looked out my bus window into the dark countryside, I prayed that Roy and I would become more like them. No college degree was required here in this quiet little valley— only honesty, kindness, and hard work.

Chapter Nine
Rough Going

The next year was a hard one. We did not have any money to spend on the ranch because everything I made went toward the ranch payments. Roy started putting the place into working condition, but it was a tough job. The fences were falling apart, and the sagebrush crowded in on all sides. He pulled sagebrush with his bare hands until they bled.

That winter was the coldest they had had in thirty-three years. The temperature dropped to a frigid twenty-eight below zero. The water froze, the pipes burst, and the house turned out to be as drafty as a barn. We were discovering the downside to ranching. I looked forward to returning to Portland each Sunday night, where I had rented a cozy little sleeping room from an elderly widow we knew.

We managed to buy a pregnant milk cow that winter, and she had her calf the day we brought her home—right in the middle of the frozen irrigation ditch. Roy found the newborn calf half dead in the icy water. He chopped the ice free and carried the calf up to the house, where we wrapped it in a tarp and laid it by the fireplace. Miraculously, the calf survived. Its mother patiently stood watch outside our door all night. In the morning we reunited them, and the cow gratefully took charge of her baby.

Because of the intense cold, we moved seven lambs into our bathtub and kept them there for over a month. We half-filled the tub with fresh hay, left the drain open, and put side rails up to keep the lambs from jumping out. Meanwhile, Roy and I bathed in a bucket. Although it was hard saying good-bye to Roy every Sunday night, I was grateful to return to my Portland conveniences.

Appropriately, we named our place "Greenhorn Ranch." Hopefully, someday we would outgrow the name, but it would still serve as a reminder of our beginnings, As each crisis passed that first year, Roy and I patted ourselves on the back. As ignorant as we were about ranching, we were learning fast.

By the spring of 1958, we had seven Hereford cows and a conglomeration of calves, sheep, horses, and barnyard fowl. We also raised some Herefords for Ivan Saunders on a 70/30 basis. He had borrowed on his life insurance to help us get started. From our share of the calves we kept everything worth raising to build up our own herd. At the same time we raised sheep, because they were more affordable. They also bring in two paychecks a year—in the spring from their wool and in the fall from their meat. We learned that many cattlemen started out with sheep.

Two years passed, and it was clear we still needed the monthly paycheck I brought in from my drafting job with Tom Taylor. By now I was well acquainted with the bus drivers who drove me back and forth to Portland each week. We worked out a system whereby they would pick me up at the Moore Ranch each Sunday night, instead of in town. As the driver approached the ranch from upriver, he flashed his headlights. I blinked the porch light in return to let him know to pick me up. Then as he slowed to a stop I grabbed a cup of coffee for him from Mother Moore and ran out to get on the bus. The driver always saved me a double seat near the front so I could stretch out and sleep on the five-and-a-half hour trip back to Portland.

Not long after Roy had moved to the ranch, Ivan invited me to attend the Wednesday night Bible study at his church. His invitation surprised me, because I assumed only church members could attend something like that. I was still very leery of getting involved with a particular denomination, but I was excited at the opportunity to study the Bible with other people. I asked Ivan what kind of church he went to and was greatly relieved to hear it was the same denomination that had given me my Sunday School pin for perfect attendance so long ago. I had cherished that pin for years until it was finally lost in one of our many moves, but I had never lost the warm feeling I had for that church.

Ivan Saunders and his wife, Evelyn

Ivan assured me I would be welcome at the Bible study, and he was right. Everyone was very friendly and kind. They didn't seem to mind at all that I was not a member of their church. Years later I discovered that Ivan had them all praying for me long before I ever came to their studies.

I had hundreds of questions about the Bible. Since the pastor did not seem to mind, I asked them all. Soon, old-timers at the church were cornering me before the services and giving me other things to ask as well. I guess they were embarrassed to ask the questions themselves, but I had no qualms at all, only an intense desire to learn all I could about what I was reading.

As soon as the Bible study ended, I would slip out of the room and hurry home while everyone else stayed for prayer. I would have loved to stay and pray with them, but I was *sure* only members could participate in the prayer meeting. Still, each time I left the church, I hoped that someday they would ask me to stay.

Then one night, several months later, as I slipped out of the fellowship hall, Pearl, the church organist, grabbed my wrist.

"Oh, Jean," she pleaded, "why don't you ever stay for a prayer meeting?"

"Pearl!" I exclaimed as my eyes filled with tears, "why didn't someone ever ask me?"

The entire group of people gaped at me. They had no idea I thought I needed to be asked. Apparently, while I had been praying for an invitation to stay, they had been praying just as earnestly that someday I *would* stay.

Although I really did not know what was done at a prayer meeting, I was thrilled to join them. I noticed some people knelt while others remained in their seats. Glancing toward Ivan, I saw him kneel, so I did, too.

Not long afterwards, Ivan asked if I would like to have a minister visit me. I told him yes, but I was very nervous at the prospect. I didn't know anything about them, really. Did they drink coffee? Tea? Milk? Where should I have him sit?

Mrs. Williams, from whom I rented a sleeping room, offered to let me use the living room for the visit, but she wanted nothing to do with it. She went off to the kitchen to have a smoke while I flitted nervously around fluffing cushions and straightening magazines. I would have loved a cigarette, too, but felt certain it would be improper to smoke around a minister.

The first few minutes after his arrival were very awkward. He introduced himself as Reverend Jones, and I motioned him to one end of the couch while I perched at the other end. We smiled at each other and then quickly looked away. A tense, awkward silence stretched between us while I fiddled with my fingernails.

Finally, Reverend Jones cleared his throat. "Ivan tells me you've read this Bible three times from cover to cover."

"Yes, Sir, I have."

He smiled. "It's a wonderful book."

"Oh, yes, Sir, it is."

"You are a Christian, of course?"

There was a long pause. "No, Sir." I shook my head and looked down at my lap.

"You're not?" He sounded amazed. "You've read this book three times, and you're not a Christian? Why not?"

I slowly looked up at him. "I don't know how," I said simply.

He stared at me questioningly, so I continued. "Well, in some places it says, 'believe and thou shalt be saved.' Other places say you have to be baptized, and it..."

"Jean," he interrupted, "do you believe that Jesus is the son of God?"

I nodded.

"Do you believe you're a sinner?"

"Oh, yes," I assured him.

"And do you believe Jesus died for your sins?"

"Yes, but..."

"Have you asked Him to forgive you?"

"Yes..."

"Have you asked Him to come into your life?"

I looked at him in confusion. "No! I didn't know I had to." My mind was whirling now.

"Oh, Jean," he said gently, "let's kneel right now and talk to the Lord."

Immediately I dropped to my knees beside a little old platform rocker, and Reverend Jones knelt beside me.

"Oh, Lord, " I pleaded, "I didn't know I had to ask You to come in, but that is what I want. Please come into my life and forgive me of my sins. Make me clean." Tears fell unashamedly.

What a sense of love washed over me as I knelt there weeping softly. Such an overwhelming feeling of acceptance— like nothing I'd ever experienced before. As I got up and slowly sat back down on the couch, it was as if that faded old living room were bathed in a golden light. The most reverent temple in the whole world could not have felt as holy as that simple little room felt to me. This was truly holy ground.

I stared about me in wonder, not wanting to break the spell, not wanting Reverend Jones to utter a word. I didn't want anything to mar this incredible moment. I wanted it to last forever.

Reverend Jones beamed as he sat down next to me. "Jean, anyone can see from your face that you're a Christian now!" He patted my hand. "Now it's important for you to really start to live like one." With his words, the glow in the room began to fade. I wished he would stop.

"From now on you mustn't smoke, you mustn't drink, you mustn't dance or go to shows..." He kept patting my hand encouragingly.

A freezing chill crept across my shoulders as he continued. Every "mustn't" he named was like a nail being pounded into the lid of my coffin, because they were all things I did. I loved to dance; I had *taught* dancing. I smoked. I drank sometimes. And what about Roy? These were things we did together—enjoyed together! It began to feel as though I had called down total "Damnation" on my soul, not "Salvation."

Like a zombie, I walked with Reverend Jones to the door. When he left I turned to go to my room and saw Mrs. Williams standing in the kitchen doorway, shaking her head. I walked past her without speaking. In my room I sat down on my bed, engulfed in misery.

I'll read my Bible! I thought desperately, but it was as if the pages were glued shut. I finally just clutched it to my heart as tears of anguish coursed down my cheeks.

I'll pray! I thought, but as I knelt by my bed no words would come. *Why should I pray?* I wondered. *God will never hear me anyway. I'm too wicked.*

I struggled to my feet and defiantly lit a cigarette, but even that did not bring satisfaction. Crushing it out, I crawled into bed, still hugging my Bible tightly as tears continued to fall. Several times throughout the night I slipped to my knees by my bed in an attempt to pray, but every effort failed. Never before or since have I felt so alone and forsaken and miserable. Satan was really victorious that night. The next morning, my cheeks scalded from the nightlong barrage of salty tears, I dressed and walked to the bus stop. I carried my Bible, as always, but did not open it to read on the bus. The bus driver knew something was very wrong and kept looking at me in his mirror, but I avoided his eyes. At work, when I walked into the office, Ivan looked up smiling, expecting to see a radiant, brand-new Christian. One brief glance and his smile disappeared.

"Jean!" he said, in dismay. "What on earth happened?"

"Ivan, you leave me alone!" I said flatly. "Leave me and my Bible alone."

At Ivan's insistence, I told him what had happened the night before, and a tremendous sadness filled his eyes as he listened.

"Oh, Jean! It's not like that, really..."

I held my Bible up in front of me. "Leave me alone, Ivan!" I repeated. "If I hadn't read this book three times from cover to cover, I'd turn my back and never return. You leave me alone."

Turning around, I walked over to my work area. Before I sat down at my drafting table, I laid my Bible on the top right-hand corner. If I couldn't read it, at least I could look at it.

There was no one I could talk to. Roy would never understand, and Ivan was the only Christian I knew. I certainly did not want to talk to that minister again, and I quit going to the Bible study at Ivan's church. The weight of condemnation that I felt crushed out my natural love of life. All weekend in Dayville, Roy kept asking me why I was so quiet. I just told him there was a lot going on at work, but he knew it was more than that.

The next three weeks dragged by in agony. Ivan honored my request to be left alone, but quietly continued to live out his Christianity in front of me. He also enlisted his whole church to pray for me. I longed to have the peace he had, but was convinced that it was not possible for me. I smoked incessantly. Early one morning, as I walked to the bus stop, a little bird flew right past my face. It came so close I felt the breeze from its wing on my cheek. Startled, I stopped and watched it fly high up into a fir tree. From there my eyes moved upward to look at the heavens. It was a beautiful, pink-tinted morning with buttermilk clouds dotting the sky. Somewhere up there was God. How I longed to talk to Him. I was so lonely. I stood very still, my eyes fixed on the heavens.

"Good morning, God." The words came out quietly, hesitantly, and then I started to cry. I hugged my Bible that I still always carried. There was no place else to go but to God.

"All right, God, You can have me," I announced in wistful resignation. "Only...please don't hurt me!" After everything the minister had said, I was so afraid God would test my commitment by breaking my legs, or hurting Roy, or some other horrible thing.

I stood there looking toward the sky for several more moments. Then, having done everything I knew to do, I started walking on down the road. As I walked, the same quiet sense of love I had felt before when I knelt by the platform rocker began to creep over me, and my steps grew lighter. I kept glancing up at the sky as a beautiful new joy started to bubble up within me.

At the bus stop, I smiled at the driver as I climbed on and said good morning. He looked surprised. It had been a long time since I had spoken to him. He watched in his mirror as I sat down in my usual seat. For the first time in three weeks, I opened my Bible and started to read...and I have been reading it ever since.

Chapter Ten
Doing Things God's Way

It seemed like everything was a little better after that—a little cleaner, a little brighter and more meaningful. I seemed to enjoy work and people and the ranch more and more. I started attending the Bible studies at Ivan's church again, and he and I started coming to work fifteen or twenty minutes early to talk about the Bible or discuss any questions I might have about our midweek study sessions.

I bought other versions of the Bible, too, and was especially drawn to the King James Version. It was the first red-letter Bible I had seen, and I came racing into the office one morning to exclaim, "Ivan! The red letters are all things Jesus said!" "Ye-e-e-s," he replied calmly, although I am sure he was astounded by my lack of knowledge.

Another time I hurried in to inform Ivan that Jesus had made the world. I felt so profound to have discovered this. Again, all he said was, "Ye-e-e-s."

Every day, as I read more and more, questions sprang up, which I asked Ivan. One day, as I was reading the third chapter of Malachi, I was especially struck by the tenth verse:

"Bring ye all the tithes into the storehouse, that there may be meat in mine house, and prove me now herewith, saith the Lord of hosts, if I will not open you the windows of heaven, and pour you out a blessing, that there shall not be room enough to receive it."

I had read this verse before, but it had never really caught my attention like this. As I read it again, I thought surely it did not mean what I thought. *Did God really want me to give Him a tenth of my earnings?* I couldn't possibly do that! It took every penny I made to help float the ranch. Half the time I went without lunch during the week just to save a little extra. I quickly moved on to another chapter, determined to put the verse out of my mind, but it wouldn't go away. I could just imagine Roy's reaction if I came home and told him I had decided to start tithing. We'd had a discussion years before about giving money to churches, and he'd made his feelings quite clear. "I earn my money!" he'd proclaimed vehemently. "Let the church earn theirs!"

Finally I went to visit Reverend Enns, the pastor of Ivan's church. He was very easy to talk to and, as usual, welcomed me into his study. When I sat down, facing him across his desk, he asked me what my problem was. "Malachi 3:10," I stated.

He stared at me a moment then got up and stood looking out the window. "What about Malachi 3:10, Jean?"

"Well, it says I'm supposed to tithe, and I can't! I use every dime for the ranch."

"Did I say you have to tithe, Jean?"

"Malachi 3:10 says I do!"

Reverend Enns picked up a book off his desk and walked to his office door. "Jean, you don't need to talk to me about this. You need to talk to God. Just go easy. Remember Roy is not a Christian." With that he walked out and quietly closed the door.

I was sure he'd return in a minute, but he didn't, so I sat there in frustrated silence. After several minutes had passed, I tried to pray, but the thought of tithing on finances already severely limited made me downright shaky. Finally, I left the office, my problem unresolved.

That night I knelt and prayed and read through the third chapter of Malachi again, concentrating closely on verses 8-12. No matter how I read it, the meaning stayed the same. God expected me to tithe. Sleep eluded me as I stewed all night long. There was just no way on earth I could afford to tithe, and yet that Bible verse told me I should. For two more nights I wrestled with the problem of tithing, until I finally knelt by my bed in resigned tears.

"All right, Lord. I'll tithe my wages...but You'll see. There's no way we can make it. We'll go broke..." I crawled back into bed, relieved to have come to a decision, but sure that financial failure lay dead ahead.

I tithed on my very next paycheck. Ten percent seemed like a huge amount, but I closed my eyes and put the check in an envelope and marked it for "missions." Since I wasn't a member of any specific denomination, the missions program at Ivan's church seemed like a good place for my money to go. I didn't tell Roy what I was doing, and tithed only on the money I earned. I didn't think it would be right to tithe on our ranch income since Roy had such strong, negative feelings about giving money to churches. Then I waited for calamity to set in.

It never did. As the days passed by everything knitted together serenely. There were no catastrophes, no bills that went unpaid—nothing. The next month I tithed again, and again steeled myself for calamity. Instead, I was asked to give my testimony at a Christian Women's Club, a worldwide ministry that holds monthly luncheons to introduce women to Christ. They paid an honorarium which helped ease the financial pressure. The third month two more Christian Women's Clubs invited me to speak, again paying an honorarium. God was keeping His end of the deal—the windows of heaven were beginning to open, and the blessings were starting to come. Seeing firsthand that tithing wasn't going to send us to the poorhouse, I decided I should tell Roy what I was doing. I waited until one weekend when I found him in a particularly fine, congenial mood. His eyes narrowed as he listened, and his face turned red. Raising his fist, he slammed it against the table. "I always swore we'd never do that!" he roared.

"Roy, I'm only tithing on my wages," I reasoned. "This is something I have to do." Turning quickly, I hurried out of the room before he could say anything else. For the rest of the weekend I avoided any more discussion about tithing and, to my relief, Roy never brought it up either.

Back in Portland the next week I knelt by my bed. "Lord, we're making it financially, even though I'm tithing, and I know it's because of You. From now on, any raises I get at work I'll split with You."

I didn't realize the repercussions of such an agreement. Too late, I realized that people should be very careful of promises they make to God. Things began to happen so fast after that, I could scarcely keep up with them. I received five raises in one year—the final one for one-hundred dollars a month! When that raise came through, I nearly backed off from my promise.

When I knelt to pray that night I almost said, "Lord, I *can't* split this raise—it's too much!" But after seeing just how wide God could "open the windows of heaven" for me when I was obedient to Him, I just couldn't go back on my word. Day by day I was discovering the magnificent principle of following Christ. It is impossible to outgive God. No matter how much I gave to Him, He gave even more back to me. He is still doing it today.

I had given my life to Christ now, but in spite of my desire to change, many unseemly habits still clung to me. Some were easy to break, but others, such as smoking, clung tenaciously. I tried over and over to quit, but failed miserably every time. How thankful I was that Jesus didn't base His acceptance of me on how good I was.

Still, I wanted my life to reflect Christ, and because Jesus said we should, I wanted to be baptized. Unable to fully grasp the magnitude of God's mercy, I thought I needed to clean up my life first and get rid of bad habits, so that I would feel good enough to be baptized. But no matter how hard I tried, I just could not quit smoking.

Finally I went to speak with Reverend Enns again. "I want to be baptized!" I announced abruptly as I walked into his office.

"Ye-e-e-s?"

"Well," I hesitated, "I smoke. I've been a chain smoker for thirteen years."

"Ye-e-e-s," he repeated, politely ignoring the obvious. My statement could not have come as a surprise to him.

"I've tried to quit so many times..." I continued.

He interrupted me. "Why?"

"To be cleaner for Jesus. That's why. I've waited to be baptized until I quit smoking, but I have waited so long, and I just can't seem to do it alone. I believe that if I give my cigarettes to Christ at the time I'm baptized He will help me."

"Well, then, we'll fill the baptistery!" he half shouted, smiling broadly.

The very next week I was baptized. Just before going into the church for the evening baptismal service, I stood in a shadowed corner of the yard and lit one last cigarette, hating my weakness as I did, but God seemed to assure me that he understood.

"Oh, Lord," I prayed, "I want this to be my last cigarette. I give You my word that I'll do my very best never to smoke again. Please help me." Excited and so very nervous, I stamped out that last, half-smoked cigarette and went into the church. Just before the curtains to the baptistery were opened, Reverend Enns asked me if I would say a few words to the congregation. His request caught me off guard, heightening my nervousness, but I agreed.

Standing in the baptistery, I looked out at all the people. There was dear Ivan, tears sparkling in his eyes. I saw Pearl, the organist, who had finally asked me to stay for a prayer meeting. Other faces were there, beloved faces of people who had been praying for me for so long. A feeling of warmth and belonging and help washed over me.

"I have lived until now for Jean," I said as my voice trembled. "I want to live the rest of my life for Jesus Christ."

Reverend Enns then immersed me in the water, and as he raised me up, a new determination took hold in my heart.

Three months passed with surprising ease. I knew my church family was praying for me, and I seemed to float along without any struggle. The guys at work never dreamed I would actually quit smoking. Most of them smoked, too, and had seen me light one cigarette off another many times. Now they watched to see how long my new resolve would last. I couldn't believe how easy it was. The cravings seemed so mild this time around. Then one weekend at the ranch, my golden bubble of victory burst. It was an early July morning, and Roy had already gone to the field to begin haying. I had just finished making the bed and was returning to the kitchen to complete some chores in there.

Lady, our big black Lab, was lying by the door and thumped her tail in greeting as I rounded the corner from the hall.

"Hi, Lady!" I called happily as I stepped around her. Just then I glanced across the room to the kitchen table. A package of Roy's cigarettes was lying there. Suddenly I couldn't see anything but the cigarettes. The most awful craving came over me, and I backed up against the wall feeling sick and shaky. I'd never wanted a cigarette so badly in my whole life.

If Satan has a voice, he spoke to me then. In my mind I heard a hoarse, throaty whisper. "Go ahead. Try one."

I shook my head. "No," I argued aloud. "What about my promise to God? What about Ivan and Reverend Enns?" The kitchen seemed to be full of an intense pressure. Even Lady felt it. She began to growl low in her throat, and her ruff came up as she looked furtively around the room and then at me.

The hoarse whisper came again. "Go ahead. Nobody will know. Just try one. You may not even like it anymore..." Tears spilled down my cheeks. "What about my friends?" I sobbed. "What about Jesus?"

Again the guttural voice coaxed me, and I could not seem to refuse it. I stumbled across the kitchen toward the table. I knew I was going to smoke. I ached with the craving and began to whimper like a child. Just before I reached the table, I dropped to my knees and began praying. I had not thought about praying until I was doing it.

"Oh, dear God," I sobbed. "You didn't say we wouldn't be tempted, but You did say You wouldn't let us be tempted beyond what we can take and I can't take it...so You'd better do something."

Tears streamed down my face. Lady came padding across the floor to me and licked my hands and face. Then she flattened herself against me, bristling and growling in protection. I threw my arms around her, and the kitchen felt like a battlefield. Shock waves seemed to bounce off the walls as Lady and I huddled there together on the kitchen floor.

I don't know how much time passed, but I finally became aware of a great stillness. Everything was so quiet, and I noticed that Lady's ruff was down. I patted her head. "It's all right now, Lady. Go lie down."

She walked over to her rug and laid down with her head between her paws, watching me intently. Slowly I got up off my knees and did something I have never done before or since—I blew my nose resoundingly on my apron! I felt drained. I wiped a few remaining tears from my face as I glanced around the room. Everything was in its place. The sunlight was shining on the table. There was a pack of cigarettes lying there... I looked around again and then whirled back to face the table. Cigarettes! There was a pack of cigarettes...and I didn't even want one.

"Oh, thank You, Lord! Thank You!" I cried over and over.

Nobody will ever convince me that Jesus didn't intercede for me that morning. He was there in my kitchen. I felt His love all around me. Again I whispered, "Oh, thank You, Lord." Once and for all the battle was won. I never smoked again.

Jean and her dog, Lady

Chapter Eleven
Roy Takes Notice

After I became a Christian, my dearest wish was that Roy would become one, too. I knew I had to move carefully, however. He had been raised by strict, unrelenting parents who had forced religion on him as a child. Now he wanted nothing to do with it. Although he knew I was attending a Bible study, I never talked to him about having become a Christian. I did not tell him about being baptized, or how I had finally managed to quit smoking. Taking my cue from Ivan, I decided to live out my Christianity in front of Roy rather than talk to him about it. I had promised him I would not become a fanatic, and I wanted to keep my word. But Roy knew something was very different with me. I did not verbally lash out at him like I used to and was much more adaptable to the impromptu situations that were always cropping up at the ranch. When Roy showed up unexpectedly with branding crews, fence builders, or trappers for me to feed on a moment's notice, I graciously complied. I knew Roy was now watching me as carefully as I had once watched Ivan.

There was just one request I made of Roy after I became a Christian. I wanted to begin giving thanks at our meals. I had learned firsthand the power in such a simple act. It had led to the change in my life; maybe it would lead to a change in someone else who shared our mealtimes. Roy rubbed his chin as he considered my request for a few minutes.

"We used to do that when I was a kid," he remembered. "Okay...I guess it's all right."

From that point on I offered a prayer of thanks at every meal, and Roy's openness to this amazed me. I had assumed he would only want me to pray when we were by ourselves. However, even when we had guests or ranch hands at our dinner table, he would wait until everyone was settled and then nod in my direction.

"Jean..." he would say, indicating I should pray. I felt certain he was softening toward my Christianity and prayed that he would soon join me in this new way of life.

Then came haying season. As usual, the men who were working in the fields with Roy stayed for supper. On this particular night, as I was putting the last of the food on the table, Roy raced into the kitchen ahead of everyone and in a stage whisper asked, "Jean, do we have to say a blessing tonight?" The question caught me off guard. "Why, no, we don't have to, but..."

"Well then, don't!" He rushed on by me to wash up. His strange request wounded me. He had made it sound as if I forced us to give thanks. I could not imagine his reasoning. The men had all eaten with us before and knew we said a blessing.

I decided not to eat that night and took my plate from the table, adjusting the spaces to one less place setting. As the men seated themselves, I went to the refrigerator and pretended to be looking for something in it.

There was a long pause, and then Roy said, "Well, fellas, let's eat!" He passed a large bowl of mashed potatoes to the man next to him. The man looked at it uncomfortably and then passed it on without taking any. The potatoes went all the way around the table without anyone serving himself. The men's furtive glances in my direction were like sharp pinpricks in my back, but I continued to rummage through the refrigerator. Roy picked up the platter of fried chicken and passed it around, but again there were no takers.

My head was getting quite frosty inside the refrigerator. Finally Roy picked up the bowl of corn and said, "Well, I don't know about you, but I'm hungry." He scooped up a large portion for himself and passed it on. Slowly, awkwardly, and in complete silence, the men began to serve themselves.

It was an awful meal. I knew they had expected me to sit down with them and give thanks. They must have thought Roy and I had quarreled. Hardly a word was said throughout the entire meal, and the minute they finished, everyone left to do sudden urgent chores. Even Roy made a hasty exit to the barn.

I cleaned up the kitchen and washed the dishes. By bedtime, Roy still hadn't returned from his "chores," so I got ready for bed alone.

"He certainly doesn't seem to be in a hurry to talk to me," I fussed to myself as I brushed my hair. Well, that was just fine with me. I didn't much feel like talking to him, either. *No blessing! Why on earth had he done that?* Miserable tears wet my pillow as I pulled the covers up around me in bed.

Roy finally came in, but I pretended to be asleep. I could tell from his breathing that he lay awake for a long time. I did, too.   The next morning, I cheerfully wished him a good morning and hurried into the kitchen to prepare breakfast. After setting it on the table, I called Roy in to eat and then went back into the bedroom to make the bed. I was determined to avoid the "blessing" time. I would stay in the bedroom until I heard Roy's silverware clinking, then I would go to the table and quietly say my own blessing. I would never ask him again! Although I heard Roy sit down at the table, no other noise came from the kitchen. I waited, plumping and replumping the bed pillows until they were in danger of wearing out. "Jean!" Roy's voice was plaintive. "Will you please come out here and say the blessing so I can eat my breakfast?"

Zing! I shot through the hall and joined him at the table for prayer. Roy never explained why he hadn't wanted me to pray the night before. I don't think he really knew why, but we never mentioned the matter again.

A couple of months later we held a branding party for the two hundred yearlings we had raised. Many rodeo people and fancy ropers joined us to practice their skills on our yearlings. They were bigger than young calves and more of a challenge. We put picnic tables up in the front yard and even hung a sign up over the corral proclaiming it "The Cow Palace."

I had spent the morning preparing a feast for the crew, and rang the dinner bell at noon to call them to eat. As the men began to jingle up toward the tables, I came out with a huge urn of coffee. At the same time Roy stood up and called for quiet.

"If you men will just wait a minute while my wife sets down that coffee pot, she'll say a blessing, and then we'll eat."

I almost dropped the coffee pot! I never dreamed he'd ask for a blessing at the branding. Roy looked ten feet tall to me at that moment.

Men smashed out cigarettes and took off their hats as they awkwardly bowed their heads. For many of them, this would be the closest they'd ever get to a prayer, so I made the most of my opportunity. After dinner, several of the men mentioned my prayer as they thanked me for the dinner.

Zeb, one old-timer, told me he had never heard of a prayer being said at a branding before. "But it worked in real good, Ma'am," he said as he tipped his weathered cowboy hat to me. I was so delighted, I hugged him.

Not long after that, I began inviting different couples from Ivan's church in Portland to visit us in Dayville. Ivan and his wife, Evelyn, came first. Then his brother, Joe Dingus, came with Ivan to go hunting. Reverend Enns and other Christian friends came along slowly, usually during hunting season. Roy enjoyed their company and loved to take them hunting so he could show off his beloved ranch. One hunting season, he looked at the group of preachers and laymen gathered around our table and joked, "It's getting to be like an ecclesiastical hunting retreat around here." Everyone smiled.

Roy didn't seem to mind if I went to church, so on Sundays he dropped me off at the little church in Dayville, while he visited an elderly friend who had sold his ranch and moved into town.

One Sunday when Roy picked me up after services, we decided to take a walk before driving home. Hand in hand, we strolled along the road and crossed over the bridge at the edge of town. Halfway across we stopped and leaned over the railing to watch the water flowing beneath us.

"Jean," Roy asked after several minutes of comfortable silence. "I know you like this little church here in Dayville, but..." He paused for a moment, then took a breath. "...if I went with you, would you go to a church in John Day?"

My heart almost stopped beating. *Roy was telling me he wanted to go to church with me!* I forced my voice to be calm and matter-of-fact. "Sure, Honey. When did you have in mind?"

"How 'bout next Sunday?"

"You got yourself a date." Somehow I got the casual words out past the huge lump in my throat and quickly looked down at the river to hide the tears that were welling in my eyes. *Roy was going to church with me!* The next Sunday, we dressed early and headed for John Day, thirty-two miles east of Dayville. During the week, I had come to realize that Roy's desire to go to a church in John Day was based on self-consciousness. He was embarrassed to do something as strange as going to church in front of his friends. Dayville was a little too close and personal.

When we got into John Day we stopped at a phone booth, and I looked up "churches" in the yellow pages. I still had no idea which denomination was the best. I wanted to pick a church where Roy would feel comfortable, but I didn't know which kind that might be. Quickly scanning the list of churches, my eyes settled on the Christian Church. That had a nice generic sound to it. I copied down the address and got back in the car.

The pastor of the Christian Church turned out to be a tall, broad -shouldered man who stood eye to eye with Roy. After services, as we were leaving the building I hurriedly scribbled him a note, "Please do not call on us. This is my husband's first time to church." When Pastor Ryan shook my hand, I slipped him the piece of paper, and he palmed it as slick as any card dealer from Vegas, without even batting an eye.

The following Sunday as we again drove to John Day, I asked Roy which church he wanted to visit this time, thinking he might want to try another one.

"Let's go back to the same one. That big fella's all right! For five Sundays we went back to the Christian Church. On our sixth Sunday I again scribbled a quick note and, just as slick as before, passed it on to Pastor Ryan in the vestibule. This one said, "Maybe someone could call on us today."

Later that afternoon Roy glanced out our living room window and noticed a car coming up the driveway. As it pulled up to the house Roy exclaimed, "Jean! It's that minister from John Day!"

"Well, ask him in," I said nonchalantly, and went into the kitchen for the apple pie I "just happened" to have ready to serve. Roy seemed genuinely pleased to see Phil Ryan and held the door open to welcome him in. Phil had barely taken his seat when he asked, "Roy, why aren't you a Christian?"

I nearly jumped into the refrigerator I had just opened to get out the cream. *Lord! Make him slow down!* I pleaded. *He's moving too fast! He'll lose him!*

Roy seemed undisturbed by Phil's abrupt question, however. "Well, Phil, I'll be along one of these days. Couple a things I gotta do first." As before, my face and fingers grew chilly as I once again pretended to rummage through the refrigerator, hanging fearfully on every word they were saying. "What do you mean, 'I'll be along?'" Phil asked.

"Well, you know. There's just some things I need to take care of first..."

"Don't you suppose you might become a Christian first?" Phil reasoned. "Then God can help you with those things."

I was sure they could hear my heart pounding now. Unable to keep my head in the refrigerator any longer, I quietly closed it and busied myself at the counter, careful to stay close so I could hear everything.

"How do you become a Christian?" Roy suddenly asked Phil.

"Well, Roy, you have to answer three questions. First of all, do you believe that Jesus is the son of God?"

"Yeah, I believe that."

"Well then, do you believe you're a sinner?"

"Ain't everybody?" Roy laughed.

"Yeah, that's true, Roy, but you gotta be sorry about it. It's called repentance." I was watching Roy now, as he nodded his head, thinking over what Phil was saying. "And see, Roy, you gotta believe that Jesus died on the cross for your sins as well as everybody else's. In fact you gotta believe that if you were the only man on earth, Jesus still would have come here and died on that cross to pay for your sins."

Like a magnet, I was drawn to the table where I reached out my hand. Roy grabbed at it as if it were a lifeline. When he looked at me, I saw his eyes were brimming with tears. "I believe it, Phil."

"Oh, Roy!" I cried, as tears streamed down my face.

"Honey," Roy smiled, "you've been sitting on my shoulder for seven years..."

"Roy Zeiler! I never said a word!"

"You didn't have to," he said quietly. "I saw it in your life."

I will hang onto those words forever.

The very next Sunday Roy went forward in church to announce that he had asked Jesus to forgive him and that he wanted to be baptized. Two rows of pews were occupied by the people from Ivan's church in Portland, who had come to know Roy over the years and had been praying for just this occasion. They had driven 287 miles to be there.

I thought it was impossible for me to love Roy any more than I already did, but now that he had joined me in my love for God, our own love took on a new dimension. My respect and admiration for Roy grew even stronger as I watched him eagerly embrace the Lord. One Sunday, in the absence of one of the deacons, Roy was asked to help serve communion at church. I watched in awe as he graciously passed the silver trays of unleavened bread and juice around to the congregation. When he came to me, I looked down at his large, rough, work-worn hands that gently held the tray, and looking up at him, our eyes locked in wordless communication. I could not hold back my tears of gratitude that God, in his unfathomable, un-explainable love and mercy, had brought us to this point in our marriage.

It wasn't long after that, coming home from another church service, that Roy grabbed onto my coat sleeve as I walked into the house.

"Honey," he asked as I turned around, "do you think we're giving enough money to the Lord?"

Remembering the time Roy had pounded his fist against the table and sworn we would never tithe, I buried my head on his chest, as more tears fell in gratitude and love for this very special man who was my husband. And we gave more.

Chapter Twelve
The Burn Out!

One chilly Thursday in January 1970, Roy phoned me at work.

"Hi, Honey!" I said, surprised, but happy to hear from him. "Do you need something from Portland?"

He didn't say anything.

"Roy?"

"Are you sitting down, Jean?" His voice sounded thick and distant.

"Honey! What is it? ...Are you hurt? ...Is Lady okay?" I was trying to think of the worst things that could have happened.

"The house." His voice was completely flat.

"The house? What about the house, Roy?"

"It burned."

My knees went limp, and I grabbed a hold of my desk. "Bad?"

"As bad as it can be," he said simply. "Only the chimney's left."

His voice was so desolate, so broken. I cast around for something to say to ease his pain, and in my own shock, only one thing came to mind. "Well, at least we won't have to worry about cleaning the attic next spring!" I said with forced brightness.

He sighed into the phone, a weak chuckle.

"I'll be on the next bus out, Honey," I assured him. "I'll be there in the morning."

Hanging up the phone, I began to shake violently as I clamped my hands over my mouth. It was all gone, he had said. *Everything was gone? Fourteen year of sweat, struggle, and dreams— all gone?*

Usually I slept on the long bus ride to Dayville, but my eyes refused to close as I relived Roy's phone call over and over. I couldn't believe that we had really lost everything. *Surely he had to be wrong! Something must be left...*

Finally, at 4:30 the next morning the bus let me off in front of the Moore Ranch where Roy had said he would meet me. It was desperately cold as I walked up the sidewalk to the house and eased open the front door.

"Roy?" I whispered.

Instantly he was beside me, wrapping his strong arms around me. We clung together in silence, too devastated for words.

"How did it happen?" I asked softly.

He told me he had awakened at 2 a.m. and glanced at a picture of the "The Praying Hands" that I had hung in the hallway leading to the kitchen. The hands looked as if they were moving. Confused, he got out of bed for a closer look. Walking toward the picture, he realized the hands weren't moving, rather the glass was reflecting light from something beyond. Turning, he saw the whole side wall of the kitchen in flames.

Grabbing a blanket, he rushed to beat them down, but soon realized the fire was far too large. He grabbed the phone and called Jim Moore.

"Jim! You gotta help me! The house is on fire, and she's going to the ground. Call everyone..." The phone went dead before he could finish the sentence.

Jim called the neighboring ranchers, and soon everyone was streaming up the road. While flames leaped around them, our neighbors ran in and out of the house carrying out everything they could grab. Thanks to their heroic efforts, much of the first-floor contents was saved.

As he finished his story, Roy said he had to go back up to the place. "The big tree is still burning in the front yard, and I want to make sure the cattle stay away from it. You get some sleep, Honey, and I'll come back for you in a couple of hours."

He hugged me tightly and left. I tiptoed into the bedroom the Moores had waiting for me and snapped on the nightlight. Kneeling by the bed, I shivered from the frosty, nighttime chill of the house. With my Bible clasped against my chest I prayed.

"Oh, dear God! Give me a verse we can hold on to. We need a verse awful bad."

I opened my Bible at random and looked down at the words of Mark 1:2, which seemed to leap off the page. *"Behold, I send my messenger before thy face which shall prepare the way before thee."*

The words were a gentle ointment on my raw spirit, and I repeated them over and over as I crawled into bed, never even taking off my coat. Curling up around my Bible I fell into an exhausted sleep.

An hour later I woke up, surprisingly rested, and wandered out into the kitchen where Nancy, Jim's wife, had fresh coffee perking on the stove. Just then her little seven-year-old niece came in the front door. When she saw me, she ran over and caught and my hand.

"Jean," she said solemnly, as big tears glistened in her eyes, "there's something you ought to know..."

"What is it, Shirley?" I knelt down beside her.

"Daddy and I went up to your house a little while ago, and we found Roy sitting on a log all by himself, and he was crying so hard..."

I swallowed as I hugged the child, crushed by the image of Roy weeping over his beloved ranch. *I had to go to him...*

At that moment, Roy came in the front door looking unspeakably weary and lost. Nancy convinced him to eat some breakfast, but we ate in silence, no one able to put their thoughts into words.

As soon as he finished, Roy returned to the ranch, asking Nancy to bring me up later. It dawned on me then that Roy did not want me to see the ranch. And he did not want to be the one to show it to me, either.

A little later, immense dread made my feet leaden as I followed Nancy out to her car. Roy's reluctance to even speak made it hard. I was not at all sure I was ready for what I was about to face.

The road leading up to our place was unchanged, and for a moment I was filled with an irrational hope that the fire was not as bad as Roy said. But then, as the car crested the rise in front of our house, my chest tightened until I thought my heart would burst. Roy had not exaggerated. There was *nothing* left—not even a pile of rubble. The fire had burned everything flat.

An eerie silence hung in the air as Nancy brought the car to a stop and we climbed out. I walked over to the ring of stones that had once been the foundation of our home. Bending over, I picked up a lone china saucer from the ashes, that had somehow survived the fire's fury. It had been part of a Chinese tea set Roy had brought back from China. I shook my head in confusion, not understanding how a two-story house could be reduced to absolutely *nothing!* In these ashes lay the substance of my life. *Which part of the ashes,* I wondered, *is my little hat from Fifth Avenue?*

I looked over to the old rock chimney that was still standing, although it was lopsided now and twisted, like a surrealist painting. I thought of all the Christmases we had spent in front of that old fireplace and of the people that had been warmed and blessed by it so many times—even long before we came.

Roy walked over, and seeing the horror welling up in my eyes, followed my gaze to the chimney. A couple of neighbors helping Roy clean up paused to look at me in mute sympathy and compassion.

"Roy?" I choked, not looking at him.

"Yeah?"

"Take it down."

"Yeah." He didn't look at me, either.

Nobody said anything as I turned and headed back toward the car with Nancy, while Roy and a neighbor got a rope and lassoed the chimney. The last sound I heard as we drove away was those rocks as they came tumbling down.

Later that day, a logger I had never met before stopped by the Moore ranch to talk to me.

"I heard about your place, Ma'am, and I'm sure sorry. It ain't much, but I got a trailer you can use so you can at least be on your own land."

Accepting his kind offer, I thought of the Bible verse God had given me earlier that morning. *"I will prepare the way before you..."* That very afternoon, the logger brought his trailer up to our place.

Roy and I drove in to Dayville for dinner that night, and the cafe owner refused to let us pay for our food. When we came outside to leave, the service station attendant across the street pointed to a huge pile of bedding, a mop, broom, buckets, and other household paraphernalia piled next to our pickup.

"A couple passing through town in a camper heard about your fire. They emptied out everything they had in the camper and told me to give it to you."

I was close to tears again, but I had to smile. *"I will prepare the way before you..."*

There were many other ways that God fulfilled His promise to us as we began to put our life back together. We did not have enough insurance money to normally cover the cost of rebuilding, but the lumber market sank to rock bottom prices that winter, making it affordable even for us. The engineers at work held a linen shower for me, and they were able to purchase our new appliances and furnace for us at 40 percent of cost. Again and again, people all up and down the John Day Valley demonstrated the magnificent spirit that had made us fall in love with them in the first place. *"I will prepare the way before you..."*

It seemed like winter would never end that year as the temperature sank to, and stayed at, a chilling twenty-eight degrees below zero. One morning I awoke to find my nightgown frozen to the side of the camp trailer. Roy had to cut me loose with his knife. I peeled our potatoes in the icy water of the little creek next to the trailer, while my fingers turned blue. "If the pioneers could do it, we can do it!" I muttered to myself through clenched teeth, but I looked forward to Sunday nights when I could catch the bus back to Portland. There my life was warm, dry, and clean. But Roy never once thought of leaving the ranch—not even for a weekend.

By the following Christmas we had moved into the utility room of our new house. I had spent many long evenings and weekends drawing the plans for our Ponderosa-type ranch house, and it was shaping up nicely. I was especially proud of the massive fireplace that dominated the living room. Five-and-a-half-tons of rock had gone into building it. During its construction, I often stood in front of it and dreamed of all the people who would eventually be warmed by its fire. Bit by bit, we were putting our lives back together.

Although it would be crowded in the utility room, Roy and I still made plans for a big Christmas Day dinner. We always invited people who had no other place to go for Christmas or no family to share the day with. We decided that lack of room was no reason not to celebrate Christmas as usual.

I set a little fir tree on top of our chest freezer and decorated it and the rest of the utility room with bits of Christmas until everything looked quite festive.

As usual, it was a somewhat colorful crew that gathered around our table. One old sheepherder had just bought a new pair of false teeth. He was quite proud of them and didn't want to wear them out. At the table, he removed his new teeth, placed them carefully in his pocket, and happily gummed his way through the meal. When he was finished, he put the teeth back into his mouth and grinned broadly to show them off.

Watching him, I could imagine my mother again saying, "Jean, why can't you ever bring home nice, normal people?" But these were still the people who needed me most.

I don't think I could have made it through the year after the fire if it hadn't been for the support of the "Wild Bunch," a prayer group of six women that I met with weekly. We had little in common except for a mutual faith in the power of prayer. It was their faith and prayers that sustained me now.

The group had formed after a series of "coincidences," but looking back, I know God drew us together for some very special purposes. We saw many wonderful answers to prayer during the time we were together.

It all began one morning at a restaurant near my office in Portland. I went in there about five o'clock each morning for a bite to eat before work. As usual, when the waitress set my plate in front of me, I bowed my head to ask a blessing. On this morning, out of the corner of my eye, I noticed a large, rather sour-looking woman in a nurse's uniform sitting several stools away. She seemed to be watching me. The next day, the same woman came in again, only this time she sat one stool closer to me. On the following day she moved down yet another stool. Since we were the only ones sitting at that long section of counter each morning, I decided that she must want to sit by me, but was too shy to be straightforward about it. The next morning, to encourage her, I moved one stool in her direction. It took a week of such maneuvering before we were finally sitting side by side.

"You weren't here last Friday," she said by way of introduction on that morning.

I explained briefly that I spent three-day weekends at our ranch near Dayville.

"Oh," she nodded, soberly. "I was worried."

I learned her name was Betty and that she was a nursing supervisor. She had been watching me pray each morning before I ate, and she began to talk about God wistfully, as if He were someone she had once known long ago.

Each morning after that, Betty joined me for breakfast, and before long we were praying together before we ate. Then one Monday Betty hurried into the cafe, her dour look replaced by pure joy.

"Oh, Jean!" she cried. "It's the most wonderful thing! My son Jason and I committed our lives to Christ, yesterday!" My eyes filled with happy tears as I realized that Ivan's example of prayer, like a pebble tossed into a pool, had now won another soul to Christ.

Not long afterward, Betty asked if we could get together once a week to pray. That was the beginning of the Wild Bunch. We met in the bedroom that I rented from Bertha, an eighty-four-year-old widow, until she asked if she could join us. We were delighted. After that we met around Bertha's dining room table. Then one afternoon during our prayer time, Betty Lou Sargent, a pastor's wife I knew, phoned.

"Jean, I just happened to be in your neighborhood and remembered this is the day your little prayer group meets. Would you mind if I joined you?"

I hesitated, feeling I should ask the others' approval first.

"Jean," she said, before I could respond, "a pastor's wife never has anyone to pray with."

With that, I quickly invited her to join us, and since we already had a Betty in the group, we nicknamed her "Sarge." Sarge brought our number to four.

Later, one Sunday at the Christian Church in John Day, Pastor Phil Ryan handed me a note he had received from a former member of the church. He suggested my prayer group might want to pray for the woman, explaining that she and her family had moved to Lakeview, a small southern Oregon town. After their move the woman had become very ill. She was now recovering from brain surgery and struggling with deep depression.

Opening the folded piece of paper, I read her weakly-scrawled, desperate words:

"I used to go to church there. For God's sake, won't someone please pray for me?"

It was signed, simply, *Wanda.*

I took the note back to our prayer group, and we immediately began to pray for her, as well as send her cards and notes of encouragement. One day she wrote to us, thanking us for our prayers and asking if she, too, could become a part of our group.

"I know I will probably never meet you," she wrote, *"but if you sent me your prayer list, I could be praying with you from here in Lakeview."* And so Wanda became the fifth member of our diverse little group, where size, age, and denomination did not matter at all.

The final member of the Wild Bunch was another Betty, whom we called "Willie." She suffered from lupus, a debilitating disease that had left her bedridden in crippling pain. Since she was unable to come to us, we drove to her house, and the four of us crowded around the bed in her tiny, dark bedroom and prayed for God's healing touch on this ravished lady.

When we finished, Willie added her own whispered prayer.

"Dear Lord, Bless these ladies so much. No one has come to see me in so long. Now I feel like I am part of the human race again..."

The following week, Willie was hospitalized. As hopeless as her situation looked, the Wild Bunch began to pray desperately for her healing. For six months we prayed, not only for her healing but that she would also be physically able to join our prayer group. We claimed her very presence with us over and over.

One afternoon we grew concerned when Sarge was late to arrive for our weekly prayer session. She was never late. We finally started without her, and had been praying a short time when the doorbell rang. I slipped quietly away to answer it.

"Hi, Jean!" Sarge stood on the other side of the screen, smiling exultantly. "Can you give me a hand?"

I looked past her to the driveway where her car was parked. There stood Willie, grinning broadly as she balanced herself on the heavy metal braces surrounding her legs.

"Willie!" I screamed. "I knew you'd come!" I flew down the steps to her side, and together, Sarge and I walked her into the house. What a praise session we had that afternoon!

So now we were six: Betty, a nurse; Sarge, a pastor's wife; Bertha, an elderly widow; Wanda, an author in Lakeview whom we had never met; Willie, a homemaker; and me. We were not very structured, but each week we made a list of things to pray for, always including the name of a missionary, as well as ourselves and two or three current urgent needs. Together we claimed the promise of Matthew 18:19-20.

"Again I say unto you, That if two of you shall agree on earth as touching any thing that they shall ask, it shall be done for

them of my Father which is in heaven. For where two or three are gathered together in my name, there am I in the midst of them."

And we began to see things happen in the weeks and months that followed.

More than a year passed, and Betty and I were still meeting for breakfast each morning. One day, when we went to pay our bill, the waitress pointed to a tall man in uniform at the far end of the cafe and said he had already paid it.

We walked over to thank him, and to my surprise, his eyes filled with tears as he reached out to shake our hands.

"You don't know what you've done for my family..." Emotion prevented him from continuing.

Betty and I looked at each other in confusion, not knowing just what we had done.

"My name is Gordon Fruits, from Lakeview. My wife is Wanda. She told me you come here for breakfast each morning, and since I have business in Portland this week, I just had to come here to meet you. I can never thank you enough for what your prayers have done for Wanda, me, and our children."

We listened in delight while he told us how well Wanda was doing now. "Things were so bad before you began to pray for us." He told us that the very worst day was when his sixteen-year-old daughter had asked, "Mom, when is our family ever going to laugh and have fun like we used to?" That was the day Wanda had scribbled the note to Pastor Ryan begging for someone to pray for her.

Six months later, Wanda herself came to Portland, and we all arranged to meet at a Chinese restaurant. The five of us were sitting on a bench in the entry area waiting for Wanda to arrive when a tall, very pale woman walked through the doors. She glanced at us, and a slow smile spread across her face. Walking over, she pointed to each one of us in turn and said, "You're Jean, you're Bertha, you're Betty, you're Willie, and you're Sarge." Although she had never met us before, she named each one of us correctly. "You have been my lifeline..." she said as tears spilled down her cheeks, and we all went fishing for our hankies.

Chapter Thirteen
Here Come Da Judge!

Roy and I had planned for me to work in Portland for just a year or two until we got the ranch up and running, but it seemed like there was always something cropping up that required me to work "just a little longer." Unbelievably, nineteen years passed while I continued to commute between Portland and Dayville.

I loved my job as a draftsperson. The downtown skyline of Portland still brings a lump of pride to my throat, because I worked on so many of the buildings. Every time I drive over the beautiful Freemont Bridge that stretches across the Willamette River, I remember the long hours of engineering skills and drafting that went into it. The center span was constructed off site and floated down the river on barges to its intended location. On the day of its raising, several engineers and I gathered on the roof of our building to watch as the huge center span was raised into place. We all held our breath until it slid into position with minimum clearance—a perfect fit!

I loved being part of building a city and never really minded the weekly commute, but there were many lonely times during those nineteen years. One December evening in downtown Portland as I waited for my bus to arrive, I watched a husband and wife meet on a street corner. They smiled and kissed and walked off together arm in arm. A deep ache welled up in my chest, and I choked back tears of loneliness.

The old familiar feeling of not belonging anywhere often plagued me. It seemed that I was neither a draftsperson nor a rancher's wife. I could not participate in the weekend plans of my coworkers or the midweek events of the community of Dayville. And while everyone in Dayville knew and loved Roy, I was somewhat of an enigma to them—the woman who came and went on the Trailways Bus.

A miscarriage early in our marriage and a later tubal pregnancy had eliminated the possibility of children, so I did not even have that bond. In my very lowest moments, it seemed like all I had to show for my life was a pile of bills stamped "PAID."

Out of the blue, in the spring of 1974, some friends from the John Day church we attended asked if I would consider running for the office of Justice of the Peace for Grant County.

"I'd run for dog catcher if it could get me over here full time," I joked. I had looked for drafting or mapping work many times in John Day, but was always told I was "overqualified." No one would hire me.

All the next week, I mulled over the idea of running for the office of Justice of the Peace. To my surprise, the position required no prior experience or knowledge of the law. It didn't even require special education. Still, the more I thought about it, the more reservations I had. Finally I phoned Roy and told him I had decided against running.

"It's too late, Honey," he laughed. "They've already collected all the signatures needed for a petition, and your name is on the ballot!"

As easily as that, my political career began. I never gave a speech, shook a hand, or kissed a baby, but when the election was over and the votes were counted, I had won by a landslide. I still don't know who did all the campaigning for me.

Overnight, my "divided" life came to an end. I was leaving secure, long-standing acceptance in Portland for what felt like a leap in the dark, but at long last I would be together with Roy on our ranch.

The minute I heard that I was to be the new Justice of the Peace for Grant County, I headed for the public library, checking out as many books on court procedure and rulings as I could carry home, especially the Statutes books dealing with the Justice Courts. In a little more than two months my new career would begin, and I planned to use the time before my swearing-in ceremony to cram my head as full of law as I possibly could.

On January 9th, 1975, I was officially sworn in as Justice of the Peace for Grant County, Oregon. As soon as the ceremony ended, I was led to the courtroom where, due to the absence of the Circuit Court Judge, my first sentencing of a convicted criminal was to be held. Even if I had had a law degree to bolster my confidence, I do not think I would have been any less terrified of the task before me. When I looked into the man's eyes, the full weight of the responsibility that now was mine dropped on my heart with a somber thud.

How thankful I was for God's promise in the first chapter of James. *"If any of you lack wisdom, let him ask of God, that giveth to all men liberally (v.5)."* Every morning, before the day began, my court clerk and I met in my chambers for prayer, asking God for the wisdom He had promised.

Offical portrait of Judge Zeiler

I also relied heavily on my show-business training that had taught me the importance of "dressing the part." I ordered black judicial robes, wore my hair in an imposing upsweep, and always carried a law book or statutes of some kind when entering the courtroom.

Usually I handled misdemeanors, civil cases, traffic and game violations, small claims, and felony arraignments. However, not long after being sworn in, I had to preside over a preliminary hearing on a serious drug case involving several counties. Normally this would have been conducted by a Circuit Court Judge, but in his absence it fell to me to decide if the case should be bound over to the Grand Jury.

The Defense Attorney was counting on my inexperience to give him a loophole to get his client off. However, the District Attorney, aware of this possibility, thoroughly briefed me on procedures.

"Whatever you do, be sure to give the defendant a chance to make a statement. If you forget to do this, the whole case can be thrown out!"

How thankful I was for the long, black robe that covered my trembling knees as I walked into the Circuit Courtroom that morning. All of the D.A.'s instructions were whirling around in my head, and I was terrified I would forget some detail that would prevent justice being served.

After both sides had presented their case, I looked toward the defendant.

"Does the defendant wish to make a statement at this time?" I asked.

"Oh, balderdash!" shouted the Defense Attorney, leaping to his feet. "Judge Zeiler, you're either awfully smart or awfully dumb..."

I looked at his flushed, angry face, and realized he had been counting on my not giving the defendant a chance to speak. I drew myself to my full five-foot-four-inch height and, looking as austere as possible, declared coldly, "You might just say I'm smart enough to be dangerous!" I glared at him until his gaze broke.

"Yes, your Honor," he said meekly, and sat back down.

"I do believe there is enough evidence to bind this case over to the Grand Jury, and I so rule." I banged my gavel and strode sedately from the courtroom.

That hearing established my respect as a judge, and it held until the day I resigned eight years later.

One of the more pleasant aspects of being the Justice of the Peace was having the authority to perform marriages. During my term as judge, I performed 104 weddings, including one on horseback. I always encouraged couples to be married somewhere other than the courthouse. I did not like performing marriages in the same place where punishments were meted out.

One marriage I did not perform personally, but do take full and happy responsibility for, involved a young man who came into my court on a drug charge. John and his hugely pregnant girlfriend were just passing through town when he was arrested for possession of illegal drugs. His hair was long and greasy, his clothes tattered and filthy on the day he stood before me in justice court. After hearing the charges against him and the cross examination, I sentenced him to ten days in jail and an eighty-seven-dollar fine. It was a large fine in view of the meager unemployment benefit he existed on.

As he was led away to begin serving his time, I glanced over at his bedraggled girlfriend. Her dirty hands rested on her protruding belly as her eyes followed him forlornly out of the courtroom. I wondered where she was from and where she would stay while her boyfriend was in jail. So many "lost" people passed through my court—some I was able to help; others seemed out of reach. Something about this young woman made my heart ache.

John served his time and then made a thirty-dollar payment on his fine, promising not to leave town until it was paid off. True to his word, he and his girlfriend showed up one month later to pay the balance.

"John, I suspect you've been doing things the 'wrong way' for a long time," I said as I took his money. "But now you've served your time and paid off your fine. You owe no man anything. Why don't you try doing things the 'right way' just once?"

He nodded and turned to walk away.

"Oh, and John..." He turned back to face me.

I nodded at his girlfriend waiting just outside the door. "If she's good enough to bear your child, isn't she good enough to bear your name?"

His face turned scarlet as he stared at the floor. Saying nothing, he walked away. At the door, he glanced back at me, but still said nothing.

"Well, I tried," I muttered to myself as I gathered up my papers. I doubted I would ever see John again.

Several months later, however, when court had just ended for the day, I heard someone come pounding up the hallway stairs. The double doors swung wide open, and I looked up to see a tall, clean-cut young man standing there, grinning at me. I stared at him in confusion for a moment before recognition dawned.

"John!" I laughed.

"I married her, too!" he shouted proudly, and with that he was out the door again.

Later I heard John was doing very well for himself. He and his wife had had two more children and had both become Christians.

Several times, citations issued in my jurisdiction resulted in some interesting correspondence. One man, who had been cited for not having a lifesaving device on his boat, wrote:

> *Dear Judge Zeiler:*
> *"...I feel that this is an unnecessary ticket. First, don't police ever give warning tickets anymore? A warning would have been more than sufficient, because I did not know that you had to have a life jacket in a rubber boat in only nine feet of water..."*

I responded to his letter by replying:

"Your letter is before me, and I simply had to take time out to answer it...especially your comment about it being an unnecessary ticket because you did not know that a life jacket was required in a boat in only nine feet of water. Pray tell me just how deep the water must be to drown a man? Or better still, how tall are you? There aren't too many people who can stand with their nose above water at that depth for very long. I feel that such a citation is necessary. Once you are full of water I suppose it could be called unnecessary, but we are hoping to keep you alive for a while yet. Please remit $14.00."

Another favorite letter of mine came from a man cited for speeding:

"We had been on the road approximately seven hours, and it was 1:45 AM when we were stopped. I hadn't seen any traffic for a long time in either direction. I was tired, and with my wife seven months pregnant, a 17-month-old baby, two other adults, and a hundred pound dog in the car, I was anxious to reach my destination..."

I replied:

"I would have been a bit anxious to reach my destination, also. You were fortunate that you did not exceed 70 mph, as there is quite an increase in penalty above that speed. That 100-pound dog of yours probably held you down. I suggest you mail this court $17.00 and buy that dog a bone."

Until I became the Justice of the Peace, I had never had a driver's license. Now, at fifty-six years of age, Roy decided I should have one. Until then, he had preferred to drive me wherever I needed to go. However, my office was in Canyon City, thirty-two miles from our ranch. Driving me back and forth to work each day was taking a huge chunk out of Roy's time.

After having a friend give me a few lessons, I went to take the test. I sat in the DMV waiting room for the longest time, until finally the supervisor himself came out and announced that he would be giving me the test.

"Nobody else wants to!" he stated. "Fact is, I don't want to either. I'd be afraid to flunk you, Judge."

We both laughed nervously. "As Judge, I'd hate to *be* flunked!" I replied.

We walked out to my car and began the test. I drove very carefully, following his instructions implicitly. At one point, the supervisor ventured, "I don't want to pick on you, but you could drive just a bit more to the right, Judge Zeiler."

As I pulled back into the DMV parking lot, the Supervisor tore off the sheet of paper he had been keeping score on and handed it to me. "You have officially passed the test," he grinned, and we both sighed in relief.

When my six-year term ended, Roy and I agreed I should run for a second term in office. I was re-elected and settled into my job, fully expecting to finish another six-year term. However, soon after I took office for the second time, Roy began to experience some small, seemingly insignificant health problems. A desire to be home with him full-time began to gnaw at me, until two years into my second term, at age sixty-two, I decided to retire.

By now, the ranch was able to support us, but without my salary, we did have to make a few adjustments. Roy and I helped support several different missionaries, and as we sat down to work out a budget, it became evident we would have to cut back on the amount of money we were sending them. We both hated to do that, and prayed it would not be necessary, but no matter how we pared down our expenses, we were still $80.00 short of the amount we normally gave to missions.

My heart was heavy the first month I sat down to pay bills and had to write out smaller missions checks. As frugally as we lived, I knew the missionaries were even more frugal. They would suffer from a lesser amount.

While I began paying bills, Roy went out to the mailbox, and when he came back in, tossed an envelope my way.

Opening it, I found a pension check for $79.63. When I had retired as judge, I had drawn out all my retirement, so I felt certain the check was a mistake. Puzzled, I went to the phone to call about it.

"Mrs. Zeiler," the person on the phone explained. "you drew out all the retirement *you* had paid in. This check represents what the county paid in for you. It was invested in annuities and can't be drawn out in one lump sum. I'm sorry, but you *must* take it in these small monthly increments for the rest of your life."

Hanging up the phone, I was explaining to Roy what the person had said, when we both suddenly realized what this meant. Roy burst out laughing.

"Well, you'd think if God could raise $79.63, He could have come up with the other thirty-seven cents, too!"

Grabbing me in his arms, Roy rocked back and forth with me as we laughed together, agreeing that we could certainly squeeze out another thirty-seven cents each month. God had once again shown us His beneficence—not only would He provide for us in our retirement, but He would also take care of His missionaries.

Judge Zeiler perfoming a wedding on horseback

Chapter Fourteen
Letting Go

In 1987, Roy went in for minor surgery to remove what was thought to be a kidney stone. I was leafing through a magazine in the hospital waiting room, when I looked up to see Roy's surgeon standing in the doorway with a strange look on his face.

"What is it?" I asked, as a heavy sense of foreboding came over me.

"It's not a kidney stone." He looked grim.

A long silence followed as I stared at him.

"Is it cancer?" I forced out the words, although I somehow already knew the answer.

"I think so."

As simply as that, my life went spinning out of control again.

A biopsy confirmed the doctor's suspicions, and Roy immediately began radiation treatments. At their completion, X-rays showed more cancer. Another surgery followed, after which the doctor prescribed a protracted series of chemotherapy treatments. For that we had to go to the Cancer Treatment Center in Bend, Oregon, two-and-a-half hours west of our ranch.

Together we sat down to consider our options. Roy had many months of debilitating treatment ahead of him, and he needed to be closer to his doctors. Even when the treatments were completed, he would no longer have the stamina to run a ranch as large as ours. As devastating as the thought was, the only realistic solution was to sell our beloved Greenhorn Ranch.

Once the decision was made, we did not discuss it further; we just set our minds to the task before us. But sometimes I found Roy gazing out the window over the fields below our house, a haunted look in his eyes. My greatest sorrow was the knowledge that I could do nothing to take that look away.

We listed the ranch with a real estate agent and arranged to have an auction to sell our ranch equipment, machinery, furniture, and other belongings we would no longer be needing. In the days leading up to the auction, I worried about how Roy would handle having strangers, as well as friends, cart off his life in bits and pieces. But God was again watching out for Roy. His leg swelled up with a blood clot the day before the auction, so his brother-in-law rushed him to the hospital in Bend, and I stayed behind at the ranch.

During the auction, I sat dry-eyed in the utility room of our beautiful ranch house and watched as hordes of people swarmed over our property. Although the auction was our choice, I still felt strangely violated as, one by one, our belongings were brought to the auction block. My only comfort was that Roy was not here to see it take place. It was just about all I could do to steel myself to handle it.

The task of packing up and moving from our ranch was as draining emotionally as it was physically. Each night I fell exhausted into bed only to stare wide-eyed at the ceiling, my mind in a continual whirl. In a way I was thankful for the massive task before me. It kept me from dwelling fully on Roy's cancer, although a sickening dread hung close to the surface of my thoughts at all times.

On October 1, 1989, with the ranch now barren and our house empty, Roy and I got into our car and drove down the long road to the highway for the last time. In the rearview mirror, I watched the last thirty-three years of our lives disappear in a cloud of dust.

Hard work and stubborn dreams had turned the Greenhorn Ranch into a profitable livelihood. We had survived through droughts and a flood, been frozen out and burned out, and rebuilt. Twice, grasshoppers had eaten our crops. We had sweated, laughed, cried, fought, and won—and loved it all.

Out of sight, on the hill above the house, lay the pioneer cemetery Roy and I had cleaned up and fenced in. When we bought the ranch, it had only one grave, a young man killed by an Indian when the valley was first being settled. Now, other graves were there—among them my parents'. They had died within a short time of each other, and neither of their spouses objected to my burying them on the ranch. I had spent most of my childhood trying to get them back together; only in their death had I succeeded. I smiled, imagining their surprise on Resurrection Morn to discover they had been resting side by side all those years. This tiny cemetery was also where Roy and I would be buried. Those arrangements had been worked into the sale agreement of the ranch.

The car continued to bump its way down the long gravel driveway as other thoughts tumbled heavily through my mind. When we reached the highway and smoother driving, I took in a deep breath, exhaling slowly, and reached for Roy's hand.

"You know, Honey, this isn't the end of the world. We've built our ranch—had our dream. God has blessed us in that. Now we just have to get you well so we can come back to this valley and do it all again. It'll happen, just you wait and see."

Roy squeezed my hand in wordless response.

We found a small acreage east of Bend, just large enough to hold the six cows and one bull Roy had refused to part with. For nearly two years this was our home, as Roy submitted to a grueling regime of chemotherapy and radiation. At its conclusion, we celebrated, certain we had weathered the storm.

We started looking for a small place back in the John Day Valley, both of us eager to return to the country that had captivated our hearts so many years before. We found what we were looking for just south of Canyon City. Sitting high atop a mountain, the house had a large picture window that offered a breathtaking view of the country we loved so much. In no time at all, we had sold our place near Bend and settled into our new home on Canyon Mountain. Roy thrived there, and we really began to believe we had a new lease on life.

About four months later, however, I began to notice Roy failing. Every day my tall, strong husband seemed to grow a little weaker.

Eventually, Roy had to be hospitalized again. There, one afternoon the doctor called me out into the hall and told me that Roy had only a short time left to live. I already knew this was true, but when he spoke the words aloud, each one became a spike pounded into my heart.

As I walked back into Roy's room, he reached weakly for my hand.

"When are you taking me home, Honey?"

"Just as soon as I can," I said.

With the help of friends, I brought Roy back to our Canyon Mountain home. Our living room was now awash with the sun-brightened colors of flowers and cards, and friends came from all around to lend their support. Daily, they gathered around Roy's bed for Bible studies, fellowship, and prayer, while Roy and I smiled and held hands, savoring every moment.

One afternoon, after everyone had gone, Roy beckoned me to his side and reached for my hand.

"It's terminal, isn't it, Honey." He made it a statement, not a question.

Oh, dear God! I pleaded in desperate silence. *Give me strength. Tell me what to say!*

I clasped his hand against my chest. "Oh, Roy! We're all terminal. I could fall off the porch and beat you. What matters is how we're going to do it. We can either go laughing or crying—I'm with you all the way—however you want. It's your call, Honey."

As weak as he was, his hand gripped mine tightly, and a smile brightened his eyes. "Then let's build some more memories."

I have never loved him more than at that moment, and I've been loving Roy Zeiler for close to fifty years. Sitting down on the edge of his bed, I plumped his pillows and smoothed his hair. *Yes, Lord. Whatever time is left to us, help us build memories.*

We already had so many together—a whole lifetime of them. Reminiscing back through the years, I realized how much a part of my life he had been—almost from the beginning.

Sometimes, when we were alone and I was working around the house, I'd catch Roy's eyes following me. They would be filled with such love that my heart would almost burst. To sidestep my rush of emotion, I'd fling a pillow at him.

"Stop that, Roy!" I'd say in mock desperation. Then we'd both laugh, and the moment would pass.

One afternoon some friends dropped by with pizza, and we sat around Roy's bed visiting together quietly. After they left, Roy beckoned me over to him.

"Jean, promise me one thing," he pleaded, grasping my hand. "Don't you ever quit working for the Lord."

"Don't you worry, Honey," I assured him. "I won't."

He turned his head to gaze out the window overlooking the pond, and I went into the kitchen to get us some coffee. Carrying the cups back in, I set them down on the bedside table. Roy was still looking out the window.

"Honey?" I smiled and reached out to touch his arm, and that's when I realized he wasn't there. As simply as that, he had stepped into the presence of God.

Last picture of Roy

Epilogue

Roy's last words became the driving force of my life. *"Don't you ever quit working for the Lord."*

After his passing, I volunteered my time to OMS International, one of the mission organizations Roy and I had long supported. Through them I traveled across the world, visiting various mission fields; then I came home to raise funds for their various projects. I have stood in Russian classrooms, Colombian prisons, and Hungarian churches, and rejoiced to see the power of God's love flourishing in each place. I have knelt in England and shared a very meaningful communion service with a Russian and an English woman and felt God's presence and approval so strongly.

Now I am in my late seventies, and God is still providing outlets for my creativity by giving me murals to paint for Vacation Bible Schools or Sunday School programs. My love of drama is used every time I am invited to speak somewhere. And always, every chance I get, I tell people about Ivan, the man whose gentle, simple witness of praying over his lunch changed my life.

Shortly before I was elected Grant County Justice Court Judge and moved to the ranch, Ivan had been diagnosed with Parkinson's disease. Each time I saw him after that, it seemed his inner light had grown a little dimmer. The last time I saw Ivan was at his church in Portland. I had already taken my seat when he came stumbling down the aisle with his walker and awkwardly sat in the pew in front of me.

As the singing began, I reached out my hand to pat his shoulder. He slowly turned dull eyes toward me, but as they met mine, they brightened in gentle recognition. He brought his hand up and gripped mine where it lay against his shoulder. He was no longer able to speak, but his hand on mine said everything. He held on to me through the entire service, and at the end looked around at me one last time, then let go.

I sat there with my eyes full of tears as he struggled from his seat and stumbled back up the aisle. I thought back to a conversation we'd had shortly after I had become a Christian.

He had said, "I used to wonder if I would ever win anyone to Christ, Jean. I've never been very good at speaking about the Lord..."

I had told him then, "Ivan, you're my Andrew. We don't hear much about Andrew in the Bible, but he brought Peter, and we've heard plenty from him. Well, you brought Jean, and they'll hear plenty from me."

No, Ivan wasn't very good at speaking about Jesus, but his life said everything. And wherever I travel and share my testimony, I tell about Ivan and how his lunchtime prayers won me to Christ...and Roy...and Betty...and Jason...and Jan...and many, many others. The list is still growing...like ripples from a pebble tossed.

Order Form

Postal orders:
Mayo Mathers, 20129 Mathers Rd., Bend, OR 97701

Telephone orders: (541) 389-0743

Please send *Like a Pebble Tossed - The Legacy of a Prayer* **to**:

Name:_____

Address:_____

City:_____ State:_____

Zip:_____

Telephone: (_____) _____

Book Price: $10.00 in U.S. dollars.

Shipping: $3.00 for the first book and $2.00 for each additional
book to cover shipping and handling within US,
Canada, and Mexico. International orders add $7.00
for the first book and $3.00 for each additional book.